CONTENTS

About this Book

Is your yard pretty enough to justify the time, toil and expense that you put into it? If not, now's the time to learn from yesterday's practical homeowners. They got great results by working with nature, employing inexpensive common or native plants and developing simple common-sense methods of planning, planting and maintaining their property.

In the early 19th Century the Door Yard was a small, well kept area of grass and flowers that bordered the walk to the front door. It was usually enclosed with a picket fence to protect it from grazing farm animals. Progress brought roads and railroads and forced farmers to keep their livestock fenced. Homeowners started to spread the pretty effects of their Door Yard all around their property but the term remained for any landscaped area of the homestead.

This book is a selection of good old-time landscaping advice from 19th Centuury farm journals, garden books and seed catalogs, presented in the original words of its authors. I tried to choose the hints that will be of help in your own "Door Yard." I hope that you enjoy your reading. — Donald J. Berg

PLANNING YOUR DOOR YARD

How to Plan and Plant Your Door Yard

Your door yard must be planned. It should be convenient, neat, handsome, restful. It will need planting with trees, shrubs, herbs, and grass; but these things should not be scattered promiscuously over the place, for then they mean nothing. Every plant should have some relation to the general plan or design of the place. The place should be a picture. It should be one thing, not many things. If the design is correct and the planting is well done, all parts will be in harmony and the place will appeal to one as a whole. The first thing is to lay out the plan or design; the last thing is to select the particular kinds of plants to be used.

The one central idea in home grounds is the house. Therefore, make the house emphatic. Let it stand out boldly. Keep the center of the place open. Do not clutter it with trees, flower beds, and other distractions.

If the house is to be made emphatic, give it a flanking. Plant trees or bushes, or both, on the sides. Back it up, also, with trees. If it sets in front of a natural wood or an orchard, the effect is better. If the country is bare and bald behind it, plant tall trees there. Make as few walks and drives as possible. They are always unsightly and expensive. Let them lead to their destination by the most direct curves. Do not make them crooked, for crooked walks and drives are expensive. If possible, place the walk or drive at the side, rather than in the center; avoid cutting up the lawn.

Most of the planting should be in masses. Plants present a bolder front when standing together. A group is one thing; scattered shrubs are many things, and they divert and distract the attention. By massing, one secures endless combinations of light and shade, of color, and of form. Against the mass planting, flowers show off best; they have a background, as a picture has when it hangs on a wall. One canna or geranium standing just in front of heavy foliage makes more show than do a dozen plants when standing in the middle of the lawn; it is more easily cared for, and it does not spoil the lawn. A flower bed in the middle of the greensward spoils a lawn, as a spot soils the table cloth. Flowers at the side, or joined to the other planting, are a part of the picture; in the middle of the lawn they are only a spot of color and mean nothing except that the grower did not know where to put them.

Plants are difficult to grow in little holes in the sod. The grass takes the moisture. They are always in the way. The well-planned yard should be able to be mown with a field mower. The bushes take care of themselves. If one dies, it matters little; others fill the gaps. If pigweeds come up amongst them, little or no harm is done. They add to the variety of foliage effect. One does not feel that he must stop to dig them out. In the fall, the leaves blow off the open lawn and are held in the bushes; there they make an ideal mulch, and they need not be removed in the spring. In front of this shrubbery a space two or three feet wide may be left for flowers. Here, sow and plant with a free hand. Have sufficient poppies and hollyhocks and pinks and lilies and petunias to supply every member of the family and every neighbor. Against the background they glow like coals or lie as soft as snow.

Fill in the corners of the place. Round off the angularities. Throw a mass of herbage into the corner by the steps then you will not need to saw off the grass with a butcher knife. Plant a vine and some low plants along the foundations. You may want a tree to shade a window or a porch. Plant it.

Have an eye to the views. Build your house with reference to them, if you can. Do not plant so as to hide the good ones. Plant heavily in the direction of the offensive ones. Plant so as to obscure the barnyard; or else move the barnyard back of the barn, or clean it up. Leave the front of the barn open; you want to see it from the house.

The lawn is the canvas on which we are to paint a picture of home and comfort. In many cases the yard is already level or well graded and has a good sod, and it is not necessary to plow and reseed. It should be said that the sod on old lawns can be renewed without plowing it up. In the bare or thin places, scratch up the ground with an iron-toothed rake, apply a little fertilizer, and sow more seed. Weedy lawns are those in which the sod is poor. It may be necessary to pull out the weeds; but after they are out the land should be quickly covered with sod or they will come in again. Annual weeds, as pigweed and ragweed, can often be crowded out by merely securing a heavier sod. A little clover seed will usually be a good addition, for it supplies nitrogen and has an excellent mechanical effect on the soil.

For all such things as lilacs, mock oranges, Japan

quinces, and bushes that are found along the roadsides, two or three feet apart is about right. Some will die anyway. Cut them back one-half when they are planted. They will look thin and stiff for two or three years; but after that they will crowd the spaces full, lop over on the sod, and make a billow of green. Prepare the land well, plant carefully, and let the bushes alone.

We now come to the details — the particular kinds of plants to use. One great principle will simplify the matter: the main planting should be for foliage effects. That is, think first of giving the place a heavy border mass. Flowers are mere decorations.

Select those trees and shrubs which are the commonest, because they are cheapest, hardiest, and most likely to grow. There is no home so poor that enough plants cannot be secured, without money, for the home yard. You will find the plants in the woods, in old yards, along the fences. It is little matter if no one knows their names. What is handsomer than a tangled fence row?

Scatter in a few trees along the fence and about the buildings, particularly if the place is large and bare. Maples, basswood, ashes, buttonwood, pepperidge, oaks, beeches, birches, hickories, poplars, a few trees of pine or spruce or hemlock — any of these are excellent. If the country is bleak, a rather heavy planting of evergreens about the border, in the place of so much shrubbery, is also excellent.

Vines can be used to excellent purpose on the outbuildings or on the porches. The common wild Virginia creeper is the most serviceable. Honeysuckles, clematis, and bittersweet are also attractive. For shrubs, use the common things to be found in the woods and swales, together with roots, which can be had in every old yard. Willows, osiers, witch hazel, dogwood, wild roses, thorn apples, haws, elders, sumac, wild honeysuckles — these and others can be found in abundance. From old yards can be secured snowballs, spireas, lilacs, forsythias, mock oranges, roses, snowberries, barberries, flowering currants, and the like.

In these native shrub borders, throw some color from nursery-grown bushes if you choose. Mix in spireas, weigelas, roses, anything you like. A rare or strange plant may be introduced now and then, if there is any money to buy such things. Plant it at some conspicuous point just in front of the border, where it will show off well, be out of the way, and have some relation to the rest of the planting. Two or three purple-leaved or variegated-leaved bushes will add much spirit and verve to the place, but too many of them make the place look fussy and overdone. You can have a botanic garden of your own, even though you do not know the name of a single plant, and your home will be a picture at the same time.

By Issac Phillips, from the 1890 book, The Farmstead

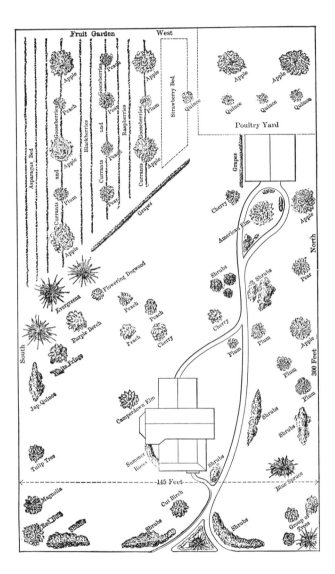

Hints on Planning Your Door Yard

From The American Agriculturist, 1874 thru 1880

The planning of your door yard should always start with a working map. If any considerable changes are to be made, it will facilitate the work surprisingly, when operations commence, to have a map drawn to a scale. The thinking and planning having all been done beforehand, no time will be lost.

So long as people insist upon having unsightly division fences, trouble must be taken to hide them. If neighbors would agree to it, a very low hedge, or a few wires, sould answer to mark the boundary, greatly to the improvement of the neighborhood. If shrubs are not desired along the fences, these may be covered with climbers of various kinds, and the rest of the border occupied by flowers. No more space should be devoted to flowers than can be well filled and well cared for. Grass is always in good taste, and can be well kept with but little trouble; a neglected flower-bed is an eye-sore.

CLIMBERS.—Provide plenty of climbers for ornamenting and covering porches, arbors, and rustic-work. Clematis, Trumpet-creeper, Honey-suckle, Wistarias, Akebia, and the like are very ornamental both in flower and foliage, and many an otherwise bare-looking spot can be easily covered by these hardy climbers.

EVERGREENS, of which a fair share should always be planted, not only for their cheerfulness in winter, but for the shelter they afford. The Norway Spruce has been found so generally successful, that we have an excess of it, to the neglect of equally useful kinds. Among evergreens, native and foreign, none exceeds in grace and beauty the Hemlock. For rapid growth and sturdy vigor, the Austrian Pine is unsurpassed. Our native pines should not be neglected, and those who would introduce variety of form and color among evergreens, will find that the nurseries offer abundant material.

FRONT YARDS IN A TOWN OR VILLAGE.—Do not attempt to reproduce a plan made for several acres, but make the best of the small area. Where all is formal, the grounds must also be so, and picturesque planting out of the question. Often a single bed of ornamental plants, or a handsome specimen plant, surrounded by grass, with a few shrubs along the boundaries, and vines at the house, are all that can be had. With only these simple materials the yard, if well kept, will be more attractive than one filled with a promiscuous lot of flowering plants.

LARGER PLACES, where there is half an acre or more between the house and the street, afford more opportunity for tasteful arrangement. The two important points are the lawn and the approaches, whether drives or walks, and they should be so planned with reference to one another, as to secure the greatest unbroken expanse of grass, and the most convenient approach to the house.

THE LAWN is the chief element of beauty in all places, whether large or small; if cut up by needless paths or by too many flower beds, its effect is frittered away, and it looks like a mere appendage to the paths and beds, rather than the ground work in which these are made.

ORNAMENTAL TREES, take as much pains in the preparation of the soil and the tree as if it were a choice fruit tree. A single specimen is in small places often better than several. The Weeping and Copper Beech, the Cut-leaved Birch, and a score of others among deciduous trees, make glorious specimens. Don't plant exactly such varieties as your neighbor has. In many of our villages one person sets the fashion and all others copy it.

SHRUBS planted in clumps are very useful in concealing boundary lines and giving a pleasing effect to the grounds. A well formed shrub standing alone is often very beautiful.

TREES.—The tendency is to plant too thickly. Young trees make but little showing at first, and over-planting is natural. For the health of the family no trees should be planted so close to the house as to exclude the light and sunshine. In planting do not copy a neighbor and thus create sameness. Do not plant large forest trees in a small yard, but select those of medium size, and attractive for flowers as well as foliage. The varieties are almost innumerable; and those from our own woods and thickets are, many times, as good as the best.

WALK AND DRIVES.—As far as possible in laying out walks let them take a direction that all will be inclined to follow, that there may be no cross-cut "sheep-paths."

WIND-BREAKS are very useful, as well as necessary in a flat country, and trees to serve this purpose should be planted wherever needed. Norway Spruce is one of the best evergreens for this purpose, as it is of rapid growth.

View of a Country Residence as frequently seen

View of the same Residence improved

Plan a Peaceful Lawn

The best expression of a lawn is that of repose; not, indeed, the repose of an unkempt meadow, but of grounds over which the hand of taste presides, and easily fashions into beauty. There should be nothing to suggest the thought of labor and cost in the making and keeping of the lawn, or of desire to attract attention and make a display. It should suggest ideas of comfort, of rest from care and toil, of freedom from excitement and hurry, of self-contained enjoyment. With this expression, the oddly shaped trees, the superabundance of statuary and the glitter of flower beds somewhat conflict. If flowers are admitted into the lawn, it should be sparingly, and they should be constant bloomers. The flower-garden proper should be disposed in a scene by itself, somewhat secluded.

From an 1865 issue of The Horticulturist Magazine

The Danger of Curved Walks

There is danger, when curves are used, of making them ungraceful or indirect, in a way to serve neither beauty or convenience. Figures A and B illustrate two examples of this kind. Tortuous walks like these prove worse than useless in one sense, for there will be a constant inclination, if not very frequent practice, to cut across the lot, as indicated by the dotted lines, instead of using the walks. People when they are in a hurry, and especially children, have little respect for long, winding, inconvenient curves, introduced for beauty, but in such cases sadly lacking it, because they lack utility.

One of the best possible remedies for the common trouble of having grass verges walked upon in private and public grounds, is to place the walks just where they are needed, and whether curved or otherwise, let them run as directly from point to point as possible, and then to make them of a material confortable to the foot. It may be stated, however, that should this bad practice be persisted

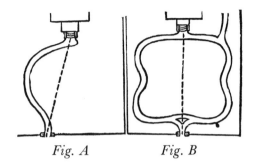

Fig. A   Fig. B

in, a protector made like a croquet arch, only much heavier and larger, and set either lengthwise, or at short distances apart crosswise, along the edge, will effectually break it up.

In Figure C it may be observed that the curves are so direct, graceful, and easy, that there would be no inducement to leave them, for gaining a more direct route from point to point.

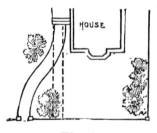

Fig. C

From the 1893 book, ORNAMENTAL GARDENING FOR AMERICANS

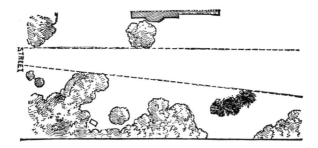

Plant for Privacy

♦ ♦ ♦

Where a beautiful garden fronts on a public highway, it is as commendable in the owner to allow passers on the street to get glimpses of the interior. But then a garden is designed chiefly for the pleasure of the owner's family and friends, and he likes to enjoy it in seclusion. It is a luxury to sit at ease, or swing in a hammock on a summer's day, and drink in the sights, sounds, and perfumes peculiar to a garden, without fear of interruption, and this seclusion should be provided for. The illustration shows how masses may be set so as to give the public some benefit of a garden, and yet render portions of it secluded.

♦ ♦ ♦

From the 1893 book, ORNAMENTAL GARDENING FOR AMERICANS

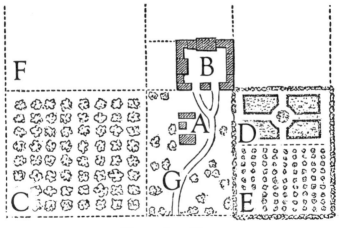

Figure 1 — Overall View

The Ideal 19th Century American Homestead

From the Register of Rural Affairs, 1857

Figure 2 — Plan

A — the house and its outbuildings; B — the barnyard; C — the orchard; D — the kitchen garden; E — the fruit garden; F — farm fields and pastures; G — the door yard.

DOOR YARD PLANTS

◆ ◆ ◆ ◆ ◆

Yesterday's practical landscapers employed a small selection of plants for the door yard. They depended on "tried and true" varieties that were hardy for their region, easy to maintain and inexpensive to purchase. If a decorative plant could also provide food, form a hedge or extend its beauty through different seasons, it was all the better. Then, as now, tender plants and exotic flowers were best left to the experts.

On the following pages you'll find descriptions of the most popular door yard plants from 19th Century farm journals and seed catalogs. You'll find additional plants mentioned in the articles on Kitchen Garden Beauty, The Door Yard in Winter and Using Native Plants. — D.J.B.

◆ ◆ ◆ ◆ ◆

Shade Trees

SILVER MAPLE (Acer dasycarpum) — This rapid-growing tree is being largely planted in many places. It is a clean tree of great beauty, and thus far has shown no tendency to disease or the attack of insects. The tendency it has of forming several main forked branches must be overcome by heading in all but the central leading branch, until it has become well established. This species thrives on all kinds of soil, but makes the best growth in a rather moist, deep soil.

NORWAY MAPLE (Acer platanoides) — While young this tree resembles somewhat the sugar-maple, but as it grows older it takes on a more rounded, massive head. The leaves are broad and thin, palmately lobed, and change to a light golden color in the autumn. It is easily transplanted and thrives in ordinarily good soil.

RED or SCARLET MAPLE (Acer rubrum) — Our common swamp or red maple, found growing throughout our Eastern, middle, and Western States, where it gives the most brilliant coloring to the landscape by its bright red flowers and fruit in the spring and the variously colored leaves in the autumn. It grows best in rather moist locations, is easily transplanted, and free from disease.

SWEET or CHERRY BIRCH (Betula lenta) — Few of our native trees are more regular or graceful in outline than this species when grown in full exposure, but it being a common native tree and producing no conspicuous flowers it has not received the attention it deserves. Trees from the woods or roadside are difficult to transplant, but when grown in the nursery are easily transplanted. They succeed best in a rather moist soil.

WHITE HICKORY or SHAGBARK (Carya alba) — On very heavy soils this tree may become a very good tree, but on light land it would be of no value. Its habit of growth is tall and upright, with bright green foliage, and is generally free from insect or fungous attack.

AMERICAN BEECH (Fagus ferruginea) — This is one of the finest American trees, but requires a cool moist soil and protection from the hot sun. It is so difficult to transplant that it is not often seen in cultivated grounds, and is rather objectionable as a lawn-tree on account of the leaves, which adhere to the branches nearly all winter. Under some conditions on a large place and among groups of evergreens the very light brown or almost white winter foliage produces pleasing effects.

WHITE ASH (Fraxinus Americana) — In growth this tree is very much like the sugar-maple with a little less of the conical form. The foliage is of a dark, rich color and free from insects and fungous pests. It is rather easily broken down by ice and wind-storms, and requires a heavy soil for its best development.

HONEY-LOCUST (Gleditschia triacanthos) — A large tree with beautiful foliage and large, often branched thorns, which cover more or less the main branches and sometimes the trunk. It varies much in shape, sometimes making very irregular growth, but it can be trained to a good form by a little judicious pruning. Compact, finely branched trees should be selected if planted on the lawn.

BLACK WALNUT (Juglans nigra) — No grander tree can be found among those native of the United States than the black walnut as occasionally seen in the Eastern States and very frequently in the West. It is difficult to transplant and requires a rather heavy soil for its best growth. It is rather slow in growth, and requires a little care to prevent the formation of low-forked main branches.

LIQUIDAMBAR or SWEET-GUM TREE (Liquidamba styracifolia) — A most beautiful tree of regular conical growth, fine dark foliage which takes on a beautiful red and yellow color in the autumn; a native of the middle and Southern States.

TULIP-TREE (Liriodendron tulipifera) — This one of our most beautiful trees, and if it could be more easily transplanted would be more largely used. The fibrous roots of this tree are very succulent and easily injured by extreme pressure or by exposure to drying winds or sun, and the greatest care must be exercised in transplanting it.

WHITE OAK (Quercus alba) — The grandest of all the oaks and one of the most common. It is rather slow in growth and wherever large trees are found, whether by the roadside or in the field, they should be preserved and the most be made of their picturesque grandeur.

PIN- or SWAMP-OAK (Quercus palustris) — This beautiful oak is only of medium size and takes the most regular pyramidal form; the leaves are deeply lobed, dark green in color, changing to a beautiful scarlet-crimson in autumn. Its acorns are small, set in a very shallow cup, and the branches stand out nearly at right angles with the trunk or with age assume a drooping form. It is a tree that should be more planted than it is.

WHITE WILLOW (Salix Alba) — The most rapid grower of all of the willows and often used to hold embankments and the soil along the borders of ponds and streams in place. While young it is regular in form and ornamental, but as it becomes older takes a more irregular growth and loses much of its beauty.

POPLARS — Very few, if any, of the poplars are of any value for permanent growth. They are very rapid in growth, easily transplanted, possessing many varying forms and colors, and useful where immediate effect is desired.

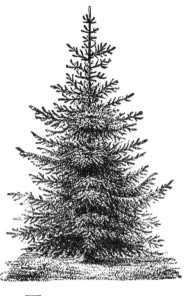

Evergreens

WHITE SPRUCE (Albies alba) — A native tree of considerable beauty of form, rapid growth, and good color. It is easily transplanted and grows in a variety of soils.

NORWAY SPRUCE (Abies excelsa) — The most rapid growing of the spruces and very beautiful while young, but after it reaches the age of 20 years and upwards its lower branches begin to fail and must be cut away. To prevent this in a measure severe heading in of the leader should be practised, which forces the growth into the lower branches. It grows rapidly even on very poor soil.

RED CEDAR (Juniperus Virginiana) — A native tree generally conical in form, found growing on dry, rocky hillsides, and is very pretty and useful for decorating such places. It takes on more or less of the brownish green, like the arbor-vitaes, during the winter.

COLORADO BLUE SPRUCE (Picea pungens) — Seedlings of this most beautiful spruce vary very much in color, some being dark green, like the Norway spruce, while others are of the most beautiful glaucous or bluish-green color. They make most beautiful lawn-trees either singly or in groups of the same species or arranged with others of varying colors.

AUSTRIAN PINE (Pinus Austriaca) — This is rather a heavy growing-tree, somewhat resembling our native pitch-pine, but with a more compact growth, longer and darker green leaves, and succeeds in a variety of soils. The most valuable of the hard pines for ornamental purposes, but should not be planted on small places.

WHITE or WEYMOUTH PINE (Pinus strobus) — This is one of the most valuable native trees for a quick growth, growing rapidly in almost any kind of soil. While young it is very beautiful, perfect in outline, and of a beautiful glaucous color, but as it reaches maturity it becomes more and more spreading and irregular, which while not unpleasant under some circumstances is not well adapted to use upon the ordinary small lawn. It is one of the most easily transplanted trees we have, whether taken from the nursery, the pastures, or woods. It stands pruning well and may be trained into a great variety of forms, although in its natural growth while young it possesses more real beauty than any close-shaven or unnaturally trained form.

AMERICAN ARBOR-VITAE (Thuya occidentalis) — A native tree of beautiful form and color while young, but soon becomes irregular and tends to lose its lower branches as it increases in age. It has produced a great many beautiful forms, some of which are much more valuable than the original type. It should not be planted where there is very great exposure to prevailing winds or where teams, persons, or animals will come in contact with it during the winter when the branches are frozen, for nothing is more destructive to its beauty than contact in zero weather.

◆ ◆ ◆ ◆ ◆

Decorative Trees

JAPANESE MAPLES (Acer polymorphum and Japonicum) — These are small-growing trees possessing a great variety of forms and coloring of foliage. They are very difficult to propagate and therefore are expensive, but in deep warm soil a little sheltered from extreme drying winds they thrive well and make most beautiful ornaments. The first-named species has produced the most varying forms, some of which have finely cut fern-like leaves, and of varying colors from dark green through many stages of variegation to the darkest red or purple.

SERVICE-BERRY or SHADBUSH (Amelanchia Canadensis) — A native tree of small size that produces the most beautiful mass of pure white flowers very early in the spring before any but the fruit-trees are in bloom. It is perfectly hardy, but is liable to be attacked by the apple-borer and must have frequent attention to prevent injury by this insect. It succeeds best in rather sheltered locations, and "though a native" deserves much more frequent use.

CANOE-BIRCH (Betula papyracea) — There is scarcely a more beautiful or easily grown tree than the canoe-birch. It succeeds in nearly all kinds of soil and is transplanted without much difficulty if trees of too large size are not attempted, those of 1 to 1½ inches in diameter being the best. It is especially beautiful when planted among evergreens or in contrast with trees and shrubs with bright yellow or red shoots for winter effect.

AMERICAN WHITE or GRAY BIRCH (Betula populifolia) — A very pretty tree when grown with a single trunk or in the group or clumps it so naturally makes. It is easily transplanted while small and grows well in the poorest kinds of soil. In transplanting large trees, i.e., from 1 to 3 inches in diameter, the trunk should be cut down to the ground and one or more shoots be allowed to grow as desired. This treatment gives a vigorous straight growth that may be put into any shape desired and the growth is very rapid.

FLOWERING DOGWOOD (Cornus Florida) — This small tree requires some protection from the hot sun and drying winds of winter to reach its greatest perfection. In full exposure the large white bracts about the flowers, the ornamental part of the blossoms, are often injured, but under the shade of larger trees, on the north slope of a hill or in the shade of buildings and in rather moist soil, it becomes one of the most beautiful of our native small trees. The pink or red form of this species is also very beautiful and valuable.

MULBERRY (Morus alba and rubra) — The mulberry is a tree of good form, with bright green foliage that is ornamental, and many persons are fond of the fruit.

WEEPING TREES — Few more beautiful objects can be seen than some of the many weeping trees that are now being offered by nearly all of our nurserymen. They possess beauty of form, grace in outline, and often produce beautiful flowers. They are especially adapted to planting upon the lawn. Most of the trees of this type are grafted upon other stocks, which in many cases results in a smaller or slower growth and adds very much to their cost.

Barberry

Hedge Plants

COMMON BARBERRY (Berberis vulgaris) — This may be used as an ornamental hedge and when grown of large size becomes protective. The more strong branches that can be secured at the start of the hedge the better. Close pruning will not give as good results with this species as the more natural growth of the bush obtained by cutting out here and there a cane to correct the form of each shrub and to cause it to thicken up and branch low.

HONEY-LOCUST (Gleditchia triacanthos) — None of our deciduous trees makes a hedge that is sure to turn animals or the small boy so effectually as this, when properly treated. As with most trees or large-growing shrubs, severe pruning is required to give them the strong growth of numerous branches at the base, and then each succeeding year if it be cut back from six inches to one foot longer than the last it soon forms a dense mass of strong shoots near the ground, covered with numerous branching spines.

PRIVET (Ligustrum vulgare) — A neat, compact shrub, that stands pruning perhaps quite as well as anything we have.

BUCKTHORN (Rhamnus catharticus) — Somewhat resembling the last in habit of growth, is hardy and tough, and stands shearing well.

JAPAN ROSE (Rosa multiflora) — This very strong growing rose promises to become a valuable hedge-plant. On account of its vigor of growth and the numerous spines it will turn animals, fruit-thieves, or other trespassers, and is ornamental in flower and fruit.

FLOWERING HEDGES — Spiraeas, hydrangias, lilacs, roses, and many other flowering shrubs may be used for hedges and often very pleasing results be obtained.

Evergreen Shrubs

· · · · ·

BOXWOOD (Buxus sempervirens) — This little beautiful evergreen shrub is largely used for a low hedge or border or as specimen plants. It succeeds best in a rather moist, somewhat shaded place, but soon fails where planted in thin soil or a southern exposure. Where a low, formal outline is desired for edges of walks or beds, it serves a good purpose, but lacks the graceful natural beauty of the laurel or Mahonia.

MOUNTAIN-LAUREL (Kalmia latifolia) — One of the most beautiful evergreen shrubs in the world, found growing wild in nearly every State east of the Rockies in hilly or mountainous regions. It succeeds best in partial shade or cool northern slopes and in rather moist soil. It is difficult to transplant, and if taken from the fields or woods only small plants must be used and these must be dug with a considerable bog of earth upon the roots. If planted in a very much exposed situation, protection of pine boughs should be given during the winter.

AMERICAN HOLLY (Ilex opaca) — A native shrub with leaves and berries closely resembling the European holly. In exposed places north of Washington, D. C., the leaves turn dark brown during the winter and are often injured by the hot sun. Should be planted in shelter, shaded from the hot sun and protected during the winter with pine boughs.

MOUNTAIN-RHODODENDRON (Rhododendron Catawbiense) — The most showy of all of the flowering shrubs when in bloom and during the winter on account of its large dark green leaves. It succeeds best in a rather moist, fibrous soil, but does well in almost any kind if it is made porous, not too dry, and if the plants are sheltered from the burning sun during the winter. While young especially, pine boughs or some other protection should be put up around them to keep the leaves from burning and to keep off fierce drying winds.

Flowering Shrubs

GOLDEN-BELL or FORSYTHIA (Forsythia viridissima) — The brightest and most attractive of the very early flowering shrubs. The flowers are of the brightest yellow and produced all over the young branches. The shoots are prefectly hardy, but in seasons when the peach-buds are destroyed by cold the flower-buds suffer and at the North fail to produce flowers.

ROSE OF SHARON (Hibiscus Syriacus) — This shrub, while not perfectly hardy north of New York City, is valuable on account of its large showy flowers, which open in August and September. If grown slowly in the border or lawn, it lives to considerable age and makes a very large shrub or small tree. The flowers vary in color from pure white to the darkest crimson and with many beautiful varieties of striped or mixed colors.

TARTARIAN HONEYSUCKLE (Lonicera Tartarica) — Some of the more billiantly colored flowered varieties of this species are very desirable. It makes a very large, upright shrub, with pink or yellow blossoms that are followed by bright scarlet berries.

RED-FRUITED ELDER (Sambucus pubens) — A native shrub, ornamental both in flower and in fruit. Berries in large clusters and bright red.

BRIDAL-WREATH SPIRAEA (Spirarea prunifolia) — One of the oldest and most hardy of the spiraeas and very largely planted. It produces long, slender branches that in the spring are covered with beautiful white double flowers. These branches may be bent around so as to form a very perfect wreath, whence the name. It has the habit of producing very few lateral branches, so that severe pruning should be given to a few of the strongest canes after blooming in the spring. Never prune the spiraeas in the spring before blooming if an abundance of flowers is desired. Like all the other species of this genus, the flowers last but a short time.

ROSE-FLOWERED WEIGELA (Diervilla rosea) — While young this beautiful shrub is very satisfactory, but after a few years' growth it becomes irregular in outline. To overcome this tendency some of the old wood should be cut out each year after flowering, which will result in the growth of young vigorous shoots that will produce an abundance of large flowers.

COMMON LILAC (Syringa vulgaris) — This is a very desirable shrub because of its hardiness and the many associations connected with the old homesteads of the earlier settlers of the country. Many of the improved varieties possess more beauty than the original types and are equally hardy.

PINK AZALEA (Azalea (Rhododendron) nudiflora) — One of the most beautiful of our native shrubs and one that succeeds best in rather cool, shaded places.

RED DOGWOOD (Cornus sanguinea) — A beautiful shrub of large size and especially valuable for winter effect. The branches are bright red, and planted in contrast with low-trained golden willow with the snow for a background very beautiful results are often obtained. A group of evergreens in front of this shrub also gives a good contrast.

JAPAN QUINCE (Cydonia Japonica) — One of the most hardy and vigorous of the imported shrubs. The flowers are mostly scarlet, but varying from this through many shades of red and pink to pure white, and as they open before the leaves unfold produce very billiant effects. Its tough, hard growth makes it valuable for hedges, which are very ornamental when in blossom.

DAPHNE (Daphne mezeron) — This is the earliest bloomer of all flowering shrubs, and its close clusters of dull pink flowers, though not very large or showy, are very pretty harbingers of spring.

Climbing Vines

WOODBINE or VIRGINIA CREEPER (Ampelopsis quinquefolia) — This beautiful native vine is very useful for covering arbors, trellises, verandas, fences, half-dead trees, stumps, etc. It is a rapid grower, is beautiful in foliage and in fruit, especially in its autumnal tints. It is also free from insect or fungous attacks, but requires some support on smooth surfaces, as it reaches large size, the tendrils not being strong enough to hold up its increasing weight.

TRUMPET-CREEPER (Bignonia radicans) — Where hardy, this is a very beautiful and satisfactory climber, though it will not hold itself to the walls of buildings and trellis-supports as well as many others. North of 42° of latitude it must be protected during the winter with some light, airy covering or be grown slowly in grass borders. The trumpet-shaped flowers of a deep orange-red are borne in large clusters and form very pleasing contrasts with the dark green foliage.

VIRGIN'S BOWER or CLEMATIS (Clematis Virginiana) — A beautiful native climbing shrub, with large clusters of flowers in July followed in September by the beautiful tasselled fruit.

JAPANESE HONEYSUCKLE (Lonicera Japonica Halliana) — This vine has the advantage that it will grow under almost any condition. The flowers are yellow, changing to a pure white, and are fragrant and abundant from June to September. It should be trained to wire netting or some other support, for if allowed to lie on the ground every branch will take root and it becomes difficult to eradicate it, except by constant pulling and hoeing up of all suckers not desired. With a slight protection of leaves, straw, or pine boughs, or by the vines lying on the ground, the leaves remain perfectly green all winter, but in full exposure they turn brown during the latter part of winter and are anything but ornamental. This is a valuable shrub for covering dry or steep embankments which are difficult to cover with grass.

CHINESE WISTARIA (Wistaria sinensis) — One of the most rapid growing vines, producing large pendent panicles of light blue flowers in great profusion. It is one of the few vines that will twine around large supports, pillars of verandas, or arbors.

Roses

We may divide the varieties most commonly grown and most desirable into six groups: Bedding-roses, hybrid perpetuals, moss, climbing, Japanese, and yellow or Austrian roses. It is impossible to give a list of varieties that will succeed in all localities or under all conditions, and each grower must decide largely what varieties will be the most satisfactory for him by the success of growers in his immediate vicinity. We, however, give a list that will prove valuable under a great variety of conditions.

Bedding-roses — Bride, Bridesmaid, Etoile de Lyons, La France, Md. Plantier, Meteor.

Hybrid Perpetuals — Anne de Diesbach, Chas. Lefebvre, Gen. Jacqueminot, Mabel Morrison, Marie Beauman, Marshall P. Wilder, Mrs. John Laing, Prince C. de Rohan, Ulrich Brunner, Victor Verdier.

Moss-roses — Common Moss, Crested Moss, Adelaide, White Bath.

Climbing Roses — Baltimore Belle, Queen of Prairie, Crimson Rambler.

Japan Roses — Rosa rugosa (white and red), R. Multi-flora, Dawson's, R. Wichuriana.

Ornamental Grasses

A class of plants at once extremely attractive, interesting and highly effective. They should occupy a prominent place in every garden. The low-growing varieties make very pretty edgings; those of medium hight produce a remarkably pretty effect in mixed flower borders, beds, ferneries, etc.; whilst the tall-growing kinds have an exceedingly elegant appearance in large flower and shrubbery borders, etc.

AGROSTIS NEBULOSA, the most elegant of Ornamental Grasses; fine and feathery; very delicate

AVENA STERILIS (Animated Oat), 30 inches high

BRIZAMAXIMA, an elegant shaking grass; one of the best of the Ornamental Grasses; perfectly hardy; sow in the open ground any time in spring; one foot

BRIZOPYRUM SICULUM, new, dwarf; with shining green leaves; very pretty; eight inches

COIX LACHRYMA (Job's Tears), grows about two feet; broad corn-like leaves

LAGURUS OVATUS, dwarf; showy heads; called Hare's-tail Grass; one foot; sow early

STIPA PENNATA (Feather Grass), magnificent grass, flowering the second season. Sow in boxes, as in beds it is often mistaken for common grass and destroyed.

TRYCHOLAENA ROSEA, a very beautiful rose-tinted grass; two feet

Dutch Bulbs

Dutch bulbs include hyacinths (Hyancinthus orientalis), tulips (Tulipa Gesneriana), crocus (Crocus sp.), narcissus, daffodils, and jonquils (Narcissus sp.). Few plants give more beauty for the labor and expense involved than beds of these early-blooming plants. Most of these bulbs are grown in Holland, whence the name. They are especially desirable on the lawn or in borders along the walks and near the house. For the best success the bed should be made deep and rich in August or September, and the bulbs be planted from 4 to 6 inches deep as soon as they can be obtained in the fall. A heavy covering of coarse manure on the bed just before the ground freezes will keep out the frost and hasten the time of blooming in the spring. This covering should be removed as soon as the snow disappears in the spring, otherwise the tops may start so as to be much injured when uncovered.

Beds of hyacinths, tulips, or crocus planted by themselves are often more satisfactory than in mixed beds, unless the quantity of each is small, when the mixed bed may be better.

Gladiolus are tender bulbs, used for summer decoration, and require but little care and give a large amount of showy blossoms.

From the 1899 book, Landscape Gardening

Favorite Door Yard Flowers

ANTIRRHINUM or Snap-Dragon, slow, but satisfactory. ASTERS; indispensable for late summer and autumn. Many sorts are in the catalogues; Paeony-flowered, Ranunculus-flowered, and Giant Emperor, are good, as are many others. CLARKIAS; all pretty. CONVOLVULUS MINOR; fine. DIANTHUS or Pinks; the Chinese sorts are good. GILIAS; small, but pretty when grown in masses. MARTYNIA; those with colored flowers are showy in a large garden, and the fruit is good for pickles. MARIGOLDS; the bronze and striped sorts are good, when they come true from seed, which is not always. MIGNONETTE; grown for fragrance only. NEMOPHILAS or Love-grove; all are fine in a cool and shady place. PANSY; too well known to need comment. PHLOX DRUMMONDII; this is the showy annual; it gives the best effect in masses; all colors from deep scarlet to white. PORTULACCAS; good, especially the double; all colors. PETUNIA; nothing is finer than the best sorts of this. STOCK; grown for both beauty and fragrance. TROPOEOLUM or Nasturtium; the dwarf sorts are very brilliant, yellow to deep scarlet and bronze. WHITLAVIA; fine blue, self-sowing. ZINNIA; coarse in growth and foliage, but with large and showy flowers, the double ones are fine and in great variety of colors. CANDYTUFT; white, crimson and purple sorts, are showy in the bed, and fine for bouquets; blooms all the better for cutting. These will give a good selection of reliable sorts. The list does not include all the good things, nor is it intended to discourage those who wish from trying novelties.

From The American Agriculturist, 1869

USING
NATIVE
PLANTS

From The Register of Rural Affairs, 1873

Liverwort

Some of the finest gems of the floral world may be still found in their native localities, and they are worth the effort to retain and preserve them, now that they are retreating with the disappearance of the forests. Plant them in shady places, and the walks, instead of being bare of vegetation, will become really fascinating.

We propose to name and briefly describe a few of our many wild ornamental plants which have perennial roots and will continue to grow and bloom year after year, the chief care being to prevent their being crowded out by the encroachments of other plants, or of grass and weeds. Some will take care of themselves and hold their own ground, while others need a little protecting care.

Nearly all these plants may be taken up any time after they have flowered and ceased to grow. Some, like the Hepatica and Pyrola, may be readily found by their evergreen leaves; others, like the Phloxes and Lilies, are soon lost by the dying down of their stems, and the places where they stand should therefore be marked with sticks while the flowers render them conspicuous, so that they may be easily found and dug up a few weeks afterwards.

LIVERWORT (Hepatica Triloba), is one of the very earliest flowers which appear in our woods, blooming almost as soon as the snow has gone. The leaves remain evergreen through winter, and new ones spring up after the blossoms have gone. The flowers vary in shades from nearly white to pink, purple, and almost blue. This plant grows in thin woods, and is easily transplanted to gardens, forming dense and beautiful masses of bloom either in open beds, or under the partial shade of trees. By marking plants when in flower in the woods, all the different shades may be obtained and intermixed in the garden.

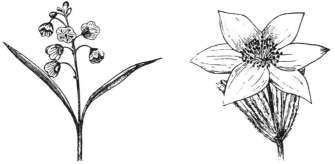

Spring Beauty   *Western Pasque Flower*

SPRING BEAUTY (Calaytonia Virginica), is one of our earliest flowering plants, appearing nearly as soon as the Hepatica, and bearing handsome pink striped blossoms. It grows freely in open garden beds or in partial shade, although not as yet generally cultivated.

WESTERN PASQUE FLOWER (Pulsatilla Nuttalliana), is found in Wisconsin and adjacent regions, and blooms very early in spring, the flowers coming up first and the leaves afterwards. As it is perfectly hardy, and grows on gravelly knolls, there is no reason why it may not be made to form handsome garden beds.

The MAYFLOWER (Epigea Repens), is one of the most delightful gems of our native woods. It generally blooms very early in the spring; has handsome, rose-colored, very fragrant flowers, and although the plant is strictly an evergreen shrub, yet its prostrate or trailing form gives it more of the character of simply a low perennial plant. Although not abundant anywhere, it is found in may localities in sandy woods, rocky soils, or along the sides of shady ravines. It would form an admirable ornament at the base or in the crevices of partial rockwork, where plenty of soil could be placed; and although somewhat difficult to transplant, it will succeed well if plenty of earth is taken with the roots, and the stems kept closely to the surface of the soil.

Mayflower

DOG'S TOOTH VIOLET (Erythronium Americanun), grows abundantly in many localities along the borders of woods in thin copses, and bears small, elegant and graceful yellow flowers, early in May, immediately following the earliest spring sorts already described. It grows in thick masses and blooms abundantly when removed to garden beds, where but little care is required for its successful growth.

BLOODROOT (Sanguinaria), bears clear white, handsome flowers, quite early in spring; the roots are thick, fleshy, prostrate, and full of red juice, whence its name; and when planted in garden beds, they need little care for years, and increase and send up a profusion of flowers every spring.

MOSS PINK (Phlox Subolata), although a native, is

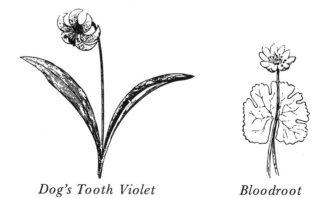

Dog's Tooth Violet   *Bloodroot*

46

already well known in ornamental gardens. The ease with which it may be propagated by dividing the rooted plants, and the little care required, except keeping it clear of grass and weeds in the garden bed, as well as its showy appearance when in dense bloom early in the season, render it a great favorite. It grows wild on dry, rocky hills and sandy banks from New York to Michigan, and farther southward.

WILD PINK (Silene Pennsylvanica), is one of the most showy of all our smaller native plants. It is found in may places throughout the country, and although not much

Moss Pink

cultivated, we have found no difficulty in obtaining brilliant displays of its flowers in garden beds in the open ground. It grows from four to eight inches high, forming dense masses of purple rose-colored blossoms. It is often found in gravelly and rocky places, and would succeed well on rockwork where not much shaded.

THE BLUE GENTIAN (Gentiana Saponaria), called also the Bottle Gentian, Soapwort Gentian, and Closed Gentian, blooms in autumn, and has conspicuous dark blue flowers, the petals of which always remain nearly closed. It grows in moist woods and along rocky streams, and is well worthy of a place in the woody flower garden on account of blooming when most other flowers have disappeared. The Gentians generally are somewhat difficult of culture, but this will succeed in a mucky, moist soil in the shade of trees.

Wild Pink

THE CLIMBING FERN (Lygodium Palmatum), has a slender wiry stem, twining closely around small shrubs and other objects. It is not a common plant, but is found in occasional localities from New England to Florida, in shaded, moist places; and its smooth, delicate form makes it a pleasing object in the wilder portion of the grounds.

Blue Gentian   *Climbing Fern*

KITCHEN GARDEN
BEAUTY

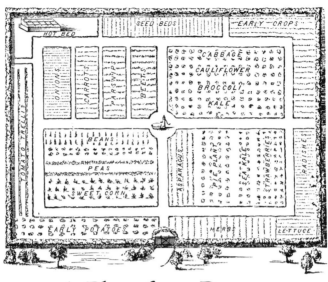

A Plan for a Pretty Kitchen Garden

By E.P. Roe, from his 1886 book, The Home Acre

In laying out a garden there are several points to be considered. The proprietor may be more desirous of securing some degree of beauty in the arrangement than of obtaining the highest condition of productiveness. If this be true, he may plan to make down its centre a wide, gravelled walk, with a grape-arbor here and there, and fruit-trees and flowers in borders on each side of the path. So far from having any objection to this arrangement, I should be inclined to adopt it myself. It would be conducive to frequent visits to the garden and to lounging in it, especially if there be rustic seats under the arbors. I am inclined to favor anything which accords with my theory that the best products of a garden are neither eaten nor sold. From such a walk down the middle of the garden the proprietor can glance at the rows of vegetables and small fruits on either side, and daily note their progress. What he loses in space and crops he gains in pleasure.

Nor does he lose much; for if the borders on each side of the path are planted with grape-vines, peach and plum trees, flowers and shrubs, the very ground he walks on becomes part of their root pasturage. As was the case with the other paths, it will be greatly to his advantage to stake it out and remove about four inches of the surface-soil. The excavation thus made should be filled with small stones or cinders, and then covered with fine gravel. A walk that shall be dry at all times is thus secured, and it will be almost wholly free from weeds. In these advantages alone one is repaid for the extra first cost.

Having made the walk, borders five feet wide can be laid out on each side of it, and the soil in these should be as rich and deep as any other parts of the garden. What shall be planted in these borders will depend largely on the tastes of the gardener; but, as has been suggested, there will assuredly be one or more shadowy grape-arbors under which the proprietor can retire to provide horticultural strategy.

A Border of Chives

From Vick's Monthly Magazine, 1881

One fine morning in June, as we passed through the vegetable garden, we were greeted with the bright pink flowers of the Chives that formed a beautiful border along the main path, a foot and more in height, bearing thousands of blooms above the masses of needle-like leaves.

The Chive is a hardy, bulbous-rooted perennial, with cylindrical leaves, seven or eight inches in length, and borne in thick tufts. The bulbs are only about half an inch in diameter. The flowers are globular and purplish. The habit of the plant is very well shown in our engraving. The bulbs should be planted in rows, four or five inches apart, and covered three inches in depth. The leaves have the flavor of the Onion family, and are cut in early spring for flavoring soups and spring salads. Cutting the leaves to the ground occasionally does no injury, but is a benefit unless done too frequently. The flowers begin to appear about the first of June, They form little or no seed, so new plants are formed from the bulbs, which can be obtained of most seedsmen at a nominal cost per bunch, the bunches being clusters of little bulbs. After growing a few years, the bulbs should be taken up, either in the spring or autumn, and reset, when, if kept free from weeds, they will soon make large bunches of unbroken borders.

Sage Flowers

From Vick's Monthly Magazine, 1881

Another ornamental plant, almost as pretty as the Salvias of our flower gardens and conservatories, is the Common Sage. The plant, or clump of plants, from which our engraving was made, was several feet in diameter, with more than a hundred spikes of its beautiful blue and purple flowers. There are few handsomer plants than the Sage when vigorous and in bloom. It is perfectly hardy here in the severest winters. Sage is usually grown from seed, though it may be propagated from slips or cuttings. Sow in hot-bed in March, or in the garden in April. Plants should be set in rows, twelve inches apart in the rows. When grown exclusively for their leaves, the Sage should not be allowed to flower, but a few plants will give all the leaves needed by a family, and flowers besides. Sage bears transplanting well. In fact, transplanting improves the form of the plant. For good, handsome plants, set them ten inches apart in a rich soil.

Kale for Foliage

From Vick's Monthly Magazine, 1881

Some of the curled Borecoles, or Kales, are as beautiful in foliage as almost any ornamental plant we are acquainted with, and, like the curled Parsleys, are admirable for garnishing; indeed, we have used the leaves for decorating large rooms, in connection with flowers, and no one suspected they were indebted for so much beauty to the vegetable garden, and to the first cousin of the Cabbage.

Kale is served like Cabbage, but it is much more hardy, and will endure considerable frost. In quite northern climates the Kale will do well in the garden until Christmas, and in milder climates Kale can be cut all through the winter. When cut frozen, they are at once placed in cold water. They do not form heads, like Cabbage, but furnish abundance of curled leaves that make the very best greens. The culture is the same as for late Cabbage.

Asparagus as an Ornament

From the National Farmers' and Housekeepers' Cyclopaedia, 1888

The old plan of sticking the plants in close beds is all wrong. There are many bits of fine soil in gardens, even the so-called pleasure grounds and hardy plant borders, where a strong clump of the common asparagus would be a great ornament, as well as of use. I shall plant a hundred or more good clumps of asparagus in our borders here, partly for its tender shoots in spring, partly for its spray for cutting during the summer and autumn months, but mainly for its feathery grace as a beautiful, hardy plant. In many a villa garden, even where good asparagus may never be seen raised in the ordinary way, a capital supply could be obtained by simply dotting a few plants here and there in borders, and on the margins of shrubberies, not only as single specimens, but as groups and masses — never, however, nearer to each other than four feet.

Vegetable Barrels

In the mid 19th Century it was common to have wooden barrels, filled with soil and planted with tomatoes, cucumbers, peppers or eggplants, right outside the kitchen door. Housewives could conveniently discard the "slops" from the sink while at the same time watering and feeding their little kitchen garden. The barrels confined the roots and kept the plants from getting leggy so they could stay small and quite ornamental. — DJB

Martynia Flowers

From an 1880 issue of Vick's Monthly Magazine

I have found Martynia as a plant both beautiful and useful for the seven or eight years that I have cultivated it. I would not put it in a conspicuous place on the lawn, but even there I have seen worse plants, but for any place a little retired I like it, and shall cultivate it as long as I have a garden. The flowers are handsome, the plant vigorous, and the seed-pods make one of the best pickles.

♦ ♦ ♦ ♦ ♦

Ornamental Egg Plants

From the 1888 book, Gardening for Pleasure

This is always an interesting vegetable to cultivate being worthy of a place as an ornamental plant, as well as being much prized for culinary use. It is a native of the tropics, and peculiarly tender. We find the seeds will not germinate freely below a temperature of seventy degrees; and even then often tardily, unless the conditions are just right. Nothing suits them so well as a warm hot-bed; and to get plants of the proper size to be set in the open ground by the end of May, the seeds should be sown early in March, and the plants potted into small pots when an inch or so in hight. But as only a dozen or two plants are needed for a family, whenever the plants can be purchased convenient-ly, it is never worth the trouble to attempt the raising of them from seeds. The best flavored variety, in our opinion, is the Black Pekin, but a pure pearly white variety is highly ornamental, and also of excellent flavor. There is also a beautiful scarlet variety, sometimes grown as a greenhouse ornament.

Curled Parsley Plants

From Vick's Monthly Magazine, 1881

If it was not for its name and the uses for which it is generally grown, there are few prettier plants than the finely-curled Parsley. The fact, however, that it is so useful seems to detract from its beauty. It made trouble for a poor gardener, who once used it freely for bouquets, when he was informed by the lady that she wished bouquets for the parlor, and not herbs for the kitchen. No one, however, can deny its beauty in the vegetable garden. The seed comes up slowly and should be sown very early, for it is perfectly hardy.

Nasturtium for Trellices

From The Family Kitchen Gardener, 1852

The beautiful Common Nasturtium has been cultivated for nearly three hundred years. Its gay colors enliven the gardens of the rich and the poor. The flowers and leaves have a sharp and warm taste, like Garden or Curled Cress; and are frequently used in salads. The seeds, when gathered young and green, on a dry day, and pickled in vinegar, form an excellent substitute for Capers, and indeed are preferable.

It is properly treated as an annual plant, and sown for the benefit of its seed, flowers and foliage, as well as for ornament. Sow the seed thinly, in rows or patches, an inch deep, about the end of March or first of April. It is not particular in regard to either soil or situation; they will thrive almost any where, if the ground is rich. The plants will run from five to fifteen feet, and require stakes or trellis-work to climb upon. There are several varieties of yellow, golden, or crimson color. The yellow stands the severity of the sun better than the crimson.

LIMA BEAN

THE
DOOR YARD
IN
WINTER

From The Register of Rural Affairs, 1877

While ornamental planting has made rapid progress in this country, there has been one department which has been much overlooked—namely, beautifying the winter landscape. The foliage of deciduous trees, and the bloom of shrubbery and herbaceous plants are gone; but in their place much may be accomplished by the soft or rich or variegated shades of evergreens; by the brilliant display afforded by masses of crimson, scarlet and purple berries, and the graceful tracery seen in leafless branches and stems of silver and golden-barked trees. In the absence of other ornament, an increased fascination is given to these objects, and even when crested with snow their brilliance is rendered the more striking.

Among the plants and shrubs which may be employed for this purpose, the following are worthy of special mention:

Red Cedar when it grows with its wild and natural luxuriance, is sometimes profusely loaded with its peculiar hoary and purple berries, which, massed among its dark foliage, present a highly ornamental appearance. By selecting among the young trees such specimens as indicate a prolific character, and removing them to suitable portions of the grounds, a very pleasing effect is produced.

Winter Berry (also known as Black Alder) is one of the most brilliant of all our native winter shrubs, and bears a profusion of scarlet berries, which continue through a large portion of winter. It is found in abundance in some of our muck swamps, and by selecting the best, they are easily and safely removed to cultivated upland soil, although flourishing in rich, mucky and rather moist land.

Red Cedar Berries

Sumac bears large, dense masses of dark crimson berries, which last through winter and into spring, and if placed in the more remote parts of the grounds, and in front of evergreens, they make a fine ornamental display.

Bittersweet displays clusters of orange-scarlet fruit, which is highly ornamental late in autumn and early in winter, and continuing longer. The opening orange-colored pods (which afterwards become white) display the brilliant scarlet berries. It is a climber, and may be trained to afford a graceful and beautiful display in winter.

Burning Bush is nearly allied to the above, and is still more ornamental when filled with its copious crimson fruit, and is scarcely equalled for the scarlet blaze which it

Winter Berries

Bittersweet

presents when well loaded with berries.

Oak-leaved Mountain Ash is to be recommended not only for its scarlet fruit, but for the beauty and symmetry of the tree, the berries hanging till cut by the frosts.

Some of the wild as well as cultivated species of Hawthorn bear showy scarlet berries, and if the most productive are selected, and made compact by pinching and cutting in, they become objects of much interest.

The common Sweet Brier, with compact training, bears an abundance of red berries, which continue into winter.

The common and purple Barberry bears beautiful racemes of berries, the former scarlet, the latter crimson purple, continuing to hang until spring.

The Bush Cranberry, if placed in cultivated grounds, and allowed space to grow, will bear freely of its scarlet berries, remaining through winter.

The Buffalo Berry bears profuse masses of orange-scarlet berries which continue through late autumn and into early winter. Its growth being rather straggling, it should be placed in the wilder and less formal portions of the grounds, in connection with the Pyracanta Thorn, as they somewhat resemble each other in straggling growth; the latter being partly tender, should be placed under the

Mountain Ash

Barberry

Hawthorn

shelter of evergreen trees, where its dense clusters of red berries will present a handsome display.

The Snowberry, with its clusters of snow-white fruit, should not be overlooked, although not lasting into winter.

Most of the preceding berry-producing shrubs should be placed in front of evergreens, not only for shelter, but for the strong relief afforded to their brilliant colors. As winter advances, many of them will gradually lose their gay appearance, and some will be devoured by birds, and for the latter part of winter the beauty of the landscape will depend mostly on evergreens. On grounds of limited extent, evergreen shrubs will be chiefly planted, or the smaller trees; or if larger growing sorts are introduced, they should be kept within bounds by pinching in or pruning from the outside. Shearing should be carefully avoided, as it gives trees a stiff and formal appearance, but they should be so reduced as to present an irregular and graceful outline. The intermixture of dark evergreens and brilliant berries requires an absence of formality in planting, and they are particularly adapted to an irregular surface, rocky grounds or ravines. Sufficient care and pruning should, however, be given to the latter to induce prolific bearing.

Among the evergreen ferns a few should be mentioned. The common Polypody Fern is rather small, very hardy, and will grow on or among rocks. The Hard Fern is

Polypody

common along wooded ravines and hillsides and is a large, handsome plant. The Woodwardias and Aspleniums, and several Aspidiums may be easily collected in our wild woods early in spring.

Among the trees and shrubs which contribute, by the color of their bark, to the attractions of the winter landscape, are the Golden-barked Willow, White Birch, the Golden Ash and the Red-twigged Cornus and if well relieved by a dark background of evergreens, become objects of much beauty and interest.

The leaves of the White Oak, and some other species, often remain through winter, and present various shades of red, crimson and purple. The young trees hold their leaves in rich masses; from older trees they fall in autumn.

Small ornamental undergrowth beneath the trees and larger shrubs should not be overlooked, as it gives a beautiful effect late in autumn, early in spring, and when

Hard Fern

the ground is bare of snow in winter. Evergreen shrubs like the wild Yew; such small plants, with broad, thick, evergreen leaves, as the Chimaphila, and the evergreen ferns; the whole surface carpeted with such species of moss as to give a soft, green surface, all add greatly to the effect.

Among the smaller evergreens adapted to places of limited extent and village grounds are the following:

The Mugho pine, growing fifteen or twenty feet high, with numerous ascending or creeping branches, the foliage resembling that of the Scotch pine. It is sometimes confounded with the dwarf mountain pine, but differs in shorter leaves and a more upright tree form. The Mountain dwarf pine has a more rounded growth of the tree. A very small variety of the Mugho pine grows only about two feet high. The Stone pine, although ultimately attaining thirty or forty feet, grows so slow that for many years it keeps well within bounds, and forms a neat and handsome pyramid, varied by the tufts of foliage on its outline. The Dwarf White pine is a bushy variety of the common white pine, of a compact form, growing from six to ten feet high.

There are several varieties of the Norway spruce, of various sizes, from the Pigmy Fir, a foot high, to those that become small trees. The common Norway spruce may be kept to the size of a small tree or shrub by continually cutting back; there are however two objections, one of which is the common want of skill and taste required to preserve a graceful natural form, instead of a heavy, formal or stiff figure; and the other the liability to neglect this cutting back until the tree has grown beyond the limited bounds allotted to it. The White spruce forms a handsome tree of moderate size, growing forty or fifty feet high; and there is a dwarf variety about the size of a currant bush. A more beautiful tree is the Black spruce, which has less stiffness and more grace of outline than many other spruces; it sometimes attains a height of seventy feet.

Among the larger pines, none can exceed, and few equal, the common White pine and the Austrian pine, while the native Hemlock is one of the finest of all our evergreen trees, when allowed full space to grow and develop its graceful form.

Turning again to some of the smaller evergreens, we should not omit to mention the Siberian Arborvitae, and the Red cedar and common Juniper. The Tree Box, although a slow grower, forms a beautiful broad and dense mass of green foliage, and becomes one of the best winter ornaments. Dwarf pine, a European species, is perfectly hardy, and easily transplanted, and grows in a dense rounded form ten or twelve feet high.

Among the flowers which may be made to bloom in early winter is the Christmas Rose, which, if planted under the protection of evergreens, and on the south side, facing the sun, may be often seen in bloom half hid under the snow.

Christmas Rose

For early spring blooming, even before all the snow-drifts are gone, plant the bulbs of the Snow-drop, Crocus, and Siberian Squill, in similarly sheltered places; and plant such early bloomers among the wild flowers of the woods as the Spring Beauty and Hepatica, and they will add greatly to the charms of the grounds while all the deciduous trees and shrubs are yet destitute of foliage, and buds have not begun to swell.

By a due share of attention to these winter ornaments, there is no necessity whatever for the bleak and dreary appearance of which so many complain.

HINTS

♦ ♦ ◆ ♦ ♦

If one may judge from his own experience, more is often learned by careful attention to "hints" in gardening than from elaborate treatises on the subject. The hint is generally the result of experience or observation, and suggests something really useful. Many who read the ponderous octavos of London, and Mackintosh and Downing, get only general principles from their study; but when they mingle with intelligent gardeners, or visit fine country places, they get ideas which can at once be reduced to practice.

From The Horticulturist Magazine, 1865

♦ ♦ ◆ ♦ ♦

Hints on Planting Trees

From the Horticulturist magazine, 1860

◆ ◆ ◆ ◆ ◆

Avoid dotting your grounds all over with trees set at about equal distances one from the other. The effect of such planting is tame and pointless; there is no variety to it.

◆ ◆ ◆

Avoid the temptation to use evergreens too freely.It is true that "they are green all the year round," but they are more stiff, formal, and gloomy than deciduous trees.

◆ ◆ ◆

You will save yourself some disappointment and vexation if you are careful to plant only hardy trees and shrubs, remembering that not all which are so classed in the catalogues are really hardy. It is vexatious to see some of your most prized trees cut down by the winter. As to protecting them with straw, screens, barrels, &c., this is not always effectual; and it is like the fashion which young ladies have of putting their hair in curl-papers, thus making frights of themselves for half the day, that they may have a little more fancied beauty for the other half!

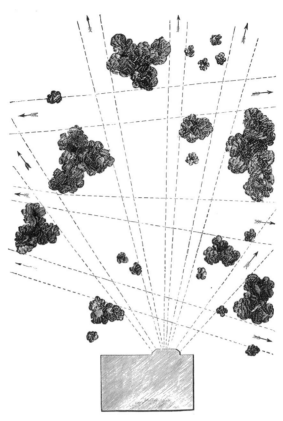

TREES AND SHRUBS PLANTED ALONG MANY RADIATING
LINES TO AFFORD VISTAS IN MANY DIRECTIONS.

So arrange your groups and masses as not to intercept interesting views of the surrounding landscape; also, so as to hide objects which are not attractive. One of the first things to be done, then, in planning your planting, is, to determine which views you wish to preserve, and which to exclude.

◆ ◆ ◆

TREES SET IN TOO FORMAL MANNER.

TREES SET IN NATURAL GROUPS.

Avoid regularity, such as planting in squares, circles, or other set figures; or so that the trees are equally distant one from another.

◆ ◆ ◆

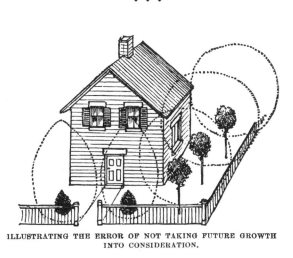

ILLUSTRATING THE ERROR OF NOT TAKING FUTURE GROWTH INTO CONSIDERATION.

Too many trees in immediate proximity to the house are to be avoided on the score of health. It is not healthy to live too much in the shade.

In arranging a group, let the tallest growing trees or shrubs be generally (not always) towards the centre of the group, and the smaller ones on the outside.

♦ ♦ ♦

In deciding upon the location and arrangement of groups, a number of poles, of different lengths, will be of assistance. By setting them up in the places where you design to put the trees, you will be assisted in imagining what will be the appearance of the group when completed.

♦ ♦ ♦

Evergreens may be planted so as to serve a useful purpose in sheltering from the cold winds, which, with us, come from the north and north-west. They are also the best to use as screens to hide disagreeable objects, because they are effectual at all seasons of the year.

By planting large-growing trees on the top of a hill you will increase its boldness as a feature in the landscape. If, on the contrary, the valley be planted and the hill be left bare, the contrary effect is produced.

◆ ◆ ◆

Do not plant too near together. Remember, that "Tall oaks from little acorns grow," and that the diminutive plants you are arranging are to become large trees. True, you might cut down a portion as they become too large, but it is hard work to order the removal of a thrifty tree, the growth of which you have been watching for years; and so, when planted too closely, trees are often permitted to grow until very much crowded and injured.

The free use of shrubs, of which the variety is now great, and of smaller trees, will tend to increase the apparent extent of your grounds. We unconsciously judge such things by comparisons.

◆ ◆ ◆

Most planters about a country home are too much afraid of the axe; yet judicious cutting is of as much importance as planting; and I have seen charming thickets shoot up into raw, lank assemblage of boles of trees without grace or comeliness, for lack of courage to cut trees at the root. For all good effects of foliage in landscape gardening — after the fifth year — the axe is quite as important an implement as the spade.

From the 1867 book, Rural Studies

◆ ◆ ◆ ◆ ◆

Fruit Trees in the Door Yard

I would like to say a word for fruit-trees, which, it seems to me, may be successfully employed in ornamental planting more extensively than they are. It is curious to observe, by the way, how prone we are to regard everything which is useful as not adapted to ornament, and even to discard it in its ornamental capacity when we discover that it is useful. Thus, tomatoes were considered highly ornamental, and were cultivated in flower-gardens for their beauty until somebody discovered that they were eatable, when they were turned out of the parlor into the kitchen at once, and one would almost as soon expect to see a bed of onions in the flower-garden now as tomatoes. Pear-trees, Cherries, Peaches, Apples, are well worth cultivation for their beauty alone. Indeed, we have few flowering trees that will compare with them. They are so useful, however, that few are willing to admit them into their strictly ornamental grounds; perhaps they are considered as working-trees, which produce something, and therefore occupy a lower grade in the social scale than the aristocratic trees which do nothing but dress themselves in fine clothes! Seriously, I suppose the objection to them is, that they are often stiff and ungraceful. This is not always so, and may be avoided by grouping and massing them with other suitable trees. Nature has used this plan with admirable effect.

From an 1860 issue of The Horticulturist magazine

♦ ♦ ♦ ♦ ♦

How to Transplant a Tree

From an 1860 issue of The Horticulturist magazine

The object is, to remove the tree from one place to another, keeping it as nearly in its present condition as possible. If, therefore, it be practicable to take up the tree with so large a ball of earth that its roots will be entirely uninjured, all that is necessary is, to deposit it in its new place, and it will experience no check in its growth. This is not commonly practicable, however, but we must come as near to it as possible. Dig up the tree carefully, take it up tenderly; do not break or bruise the roots, or suffer them to dry, for this is death to them. Put the roots into their new place as nearly as possible in their natural position — that is, in the position they were in before. This is the whole secret. It is only necessary to remember, that the roots of a tree are very delicate things. They will live a little longer out of the ground, or some substitute, than a fish will out of water, but not much. As to their texture, some of them are scarcely coarser or stronger than cobwebs. Consequently, with all our care, we cannot avoid injuring them considerably, and therefore it is necessary to remove a portion of their branches, for the top is supported by the roots, and if the latter are diminished the former must be also.

Reflect, then, upon what is the present position of the roots of the tree you are about to move; their frailty; how they are spread out and separated, one scarcely ever touching another; how the earth lies closely around them; — remember these things, and you will not need to be told how to go to work to move a tree.

The weather for transplanting, whether of table vegetables, or of trees, is the same as that for sowing. If you do this work in wet weather, or when the ground is wet, the work cannot be well done. It is no matter what the plant is, whether it be a cucumber plant, or an oak tree. It has been observed, as to seeds, that they like the earth to touch them in every part, and to lie close about them. It is the same with roots. One half of the bad growth that we see in orchards arises from negligence in planting; from tumbling the earth carelessly in upon the roots. The earth should be fine as possible; for, if it be not, part of the roots will remain untouched by the earth. If ground be wet, it cannot be fine.

If possible, therefore, transplant when the ground is not wet; but, here again, as in the case of sowing, let it be dug or deeply moved, and well broken, immediately before you transplant into it.

A WELL BALANCED EVERGREEN.

Hints on Using Evergreens

Evergreen trees are indispensable in ornamental gardening. They are especially valuable for screens and windbreaks, for a background against which to group trees with beautifully colored leaves or branches, and for winter decoration. The too abundant use of evergreens results in a sombre effect and often to an unhealthy condition if planted too close to the buildings. The limit and scope of this work will allow of the description of only the most beautiful, and those that succeed under a wide range of conditions and are most easily transplanted. Small evergreens should not be planted where persons or animals passing will brush against them continually during the winter, as they are very easily injured in this way while frozen.

Evergreens may be transplanted at almost any season of the year, but great care needs to be taken that the roots do not become dry by exposure to sun and wind, and if possible a moist day should be selected. Evergreens, like all other trees and shrubs, must have an abundance of plant-food. The annual dressing of compost should be applied to them as much as to the flowering shrubs, at least until they have become thoroughly established. Nearly all are also benefited by pruning, especially those that tend to grow into a close spiry form. This is best done in the spring before growth begins, though it may be done at any time with fair success.

From the book, Landscape Gardening, 1899

A BADLY TRAINED TREE.

♦ ♦ ♦ ♦ ♦

How to Collect and Plant Native Evergreens

Nothing is more beautiful than a well grown specimen of our common White Pine, or Weymouth Pine, as it is called. The chief obstacle to its general introduction seems to be its nativity. If it were brought from a distance and sold at a very high price, it would be more generally sought after. Then there is the common Hemlock, than which few evergreens are more beautiful. It is unfortunately rather impatient of removal, but it is worth while to take special pains to secure so fine a tree.

For planting evergreens, May is the most suitable month. They are very easily taken up, since the roots grow in a close knot about the stock. Go to a pine or hemlock grove with a team, select the smaller trees or shrubs, cut with a spade, or better an old axe, a circle large enough to include the most of the roots, and the tree may be lifted out very easily. The dirt will cling to the roots, and their growth will hardly be checked. The great trial for evergreens, taken from the woods, is the sunshine, to which they have not been accustomed. But if they are set thickly and in considerable numbers, only a few will die. Those obtained from the nurseries are acclimated and do not suffer in this way, but they are more expensive.

At any time, and especially in late planting, the greatest care should be taken to prevent the roots of evergreens from drying. They should be kept well covered from the moment they are out of the ground till they are replanted. Where it is practicable, the holes should be prepared beforehand, adding peaty earth if the soil is of a sandy character, and then wait for a cloudy day upon which to take up the trees from the nursery. Large stones laid over the roots are better than stakes; besides holding the tree in place they will act as a mulch to prevent the soil from drying out.

From The American Agriculturist, 1866 and 1879

Plant Evergreens for Shelter

From The American Agriculturist, 1866

Screens are planted for two purposes: the concealment of objects offensive to the taste, and the shelter of buildings, gardens and orchards from the winds. It is of screens as a shelter that we purpose to say a word here. The importance of shelter in a northern climate is but little understood. It answers several economic as well as esthetic purposes. No country home has its appropriate surroundings until evergreens are planted. It is cheerless and desolate in winter—it lacks the highest charm in summer. By the shelter of evergreens, we may change the temperature of the seasons, and give gardens and orchards the climate of regions four or five degrees further south. The violence of the prevailing winds may be completely broken, so that the thermometer will not sink so low in winter, and the snow, instead of drifting in heaps and leaving many places bare, will spread its soft covering evenly over all delicate plants and preserve them. Many of the difficulties with which the gardener and orchardist have to contend, may be obviated by the shelter of trees. One reason why grapes and other small fruits do better in cities and villages than in the country, is the fact that they have the shelter of yards and buildings. Train an Isabella upon a trellis in an open field, and you may not get a crop once in five years. Put it upon the south or east side of a building, and, with suitable feeding and pruning, the crop is generally as sure as that of Indian corn.

One of the best examples of the ameliorating influences of shelter upon climate that has ever fallen under our observation, was upon the farm of the late Judge Meech, of Shelburne, Vt. His homestead was near the shores of Champlain, and swept by the severe lake winds in the winter and spring. He inclosed about two acres with a screen of American Arbor Vitae, that being the most common evergreen of the region. Within this inclosure he could raise the grape, the peach, and other fruits that would not mature outside.

There are several varieties of evergreens that make perfect shelter , and we should be governed in their selection mainly by the cost of the plants and the facility of transplanting. We put at the head of the list the Norway Spruce, and this conifer has been so extensively imported for the last dozen years or more, that almost every well established nursery has a large stock, and they are as cheap as any other tree. Many nurseries have evergreen trees fit for no other purpose than screens, or to be cut up for stakes and poles.

The distance of planting will be determined somewhat by the size of the trees, and the immediate objects aimed at. With Norway Spruces ten or twelve feet high, an effective shelter may be made at once. We have succeeded admirably with trees of this size, losing less than five per cent—planting them so that the limbs just touched.

It is safer, however, to plant smaller trees, and closer together, even if you have to take out the alternate trees two or three years later. A screen for an apple orchard may be left to grow twenty-five or thirty feet high, and in this case the trees should be at least ten feet apart to give the requisite strength at the base.

A screen, unlike a hedge, does not require close planting, and not much shearing or attention of any kind, after it is once established.

A Common Mistake in Planting

From THE AMERICAN AGRICULTURIST, 1862

One of the greatest and commonest errors in tree-planting, is that of setting out large trees and many of them, in small areas. The home improver thinks that he wants a great variety of trees, such as he has seen on Mr. Smith's place, and at Judge Jones' great establishment. So he adds tree to tree, year after year. While they are small, they look pretty, and all goes on well. But ere long, they spread out their limbs on every side, until they meet and overlap each other, making a complete forest jungle. None of them can become well-formed trees; they grow up spindling, or lop-sided, and give little real satisfaction. And besides, what can be expected of the grass under such overhanging boughs and such a mass of tree-roots? And what of shrubs and plants? Where, too, are the views of the street, or of the surrounding country? Everyway, the practice is bad.

Here let a remedy be suggested: Set out but few trees. Plant the largest along the boundaries, and the smaller around the dwelling. Set them so as to preserve views of the neighborhood, at the best out-looks. Calculate for their growth many years ahead, and plant accordingly. Many persons plant a large number of trees in their grounds, intending, at some future day, when the trees become crowded, to thin them out. But very few persons have resolution enough to cut down a tree which has become large and thrifty, especially if it was planted by themselves.

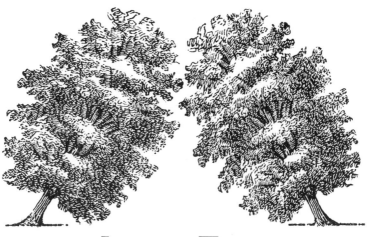

Leaning Trees

When crooked, lop-sided, leaning trees are seen in a wild forest, we call them picturesque, and let it go. But when we see them in a neighbor's orchard, (or our own), or by the roadside, or in a lawn, we say somebody is to blame, for generally it comes from sheer neglect. As to leaning trees, the history is something like this: when first transplanted from the nursery or the woods, they are straight and tall. They are set out in exposed places, and not being staked and tied up, they soon get out of the perpendicular. This is not to be wondered at, considering the smallness of the roots, and the softness of the soil. It is a very easy matter to prevent this. Let every newly planted tree be staked and tied up, using broad and soft bands to prevent chafing the bark. Or, in the lack of stakes and bands, use heaps of stones laid over the roots on the windy side, which will ballast them. In case a tree gets thrown over, it can be righted up by loosening the earth about the roots, and then drawing it up and fastening it to a stout stake. If it has stood leaning for several years, it may be necessary to use an ax on one or two obstinate roots. But by all means get every tree up straight and then keep it up.

From THE AMERICAN AGRICULTURIST, 1862

Digging for Treasure

From THE AMERICAN AGRICULTURIST, 1863

For how much money would you cut down the fruit and shade trees on your property? Every owner will, in reply, name a sum far above the cost of planting and raising them. This proves conclusively that tree planting will pay. We know of no more certain way to increase the market price and the salableness of a property, than by stocking it with trees. The satisfaction to be derived from abundance of fruit and shade, the attractiveness thereby given to the Home, and its good influence upon the family circle, these can hardly be estimated in dollars and cents.

Now is the time to make this richly paying investment. Commence in the vicinity of the dwelling. The peaches, cherries, and other stone fruits, and tender trees, will be better left until next Spring. For apples, pears, and deciduous shade trees, the best time is when the frost has nearly stripped them of leaves. They become well settled in their places during Winter, and are ready to commence growth when Spring opens. A few essential points need attention in transplanting. Large trees may be successfully transplanted by using extra care, but it is generally far preferable to take those of only a few years' growth. In a few years they will outstrip those of larger size, and be of better shape, as they need little pruning when removed.

Make the holes large enough to allow of spreading the roots to their full length, and lay them all out in the direction of growth. Set the trees at the same depth as they originally grew.

Walks

From The Register of Rural Affairs, 1865

There is no part of gardens or pleasure grounds more expressive of the character of the keeping than the walks. No matter how fine the flower beds may be, if the walks are not bounded by smooth and graceful curves, or if they are rough, irregular and unfinished, the grounds will convey unmistakably an expression of bad management. But a smooth and perfect walk on the other hand, even if carried through a wild natural shrubbery, imparts a finished air to the whole.

♦ ♦ ♦ ♦ ♦

It is essential to good appearance, that curved walks be entirely free from all appearance of angles or abruptness at any point. When the curve is made to increase or diminish, it should be done gracefully and uniformly. It is usually accomplished in practice by first drawing the plan on paper, and afterwards transferring it by measurement of its principal points to the ground. This is not difficult, if drawn accurately to a definite scale; short pegs being used to mark the points. Intermediate curves may be laid out with much accuracy, by sticking short pegs of wood into the ground at equal distances from each other, but instead of being in a straight line, let each one deviate a certain uniform distance from the right line, and a true curve will be formed. When it is desired to change from a short to a longer curve, gradually increase the distance between the pegs.

The following rules for designing curved walks should always be observed:

1. They should never follow closely a boundary fence, and where they pass near it, it should be hid by the foliage of trees, of which that of evergreens is most dense.

2. They should never bend without an obvious reason — either to avoid a change of level, a group of trees, a mass of shrubbery, a flower-bed, or to reach a distant object not lying directly before the spectator. Unmeaning curves, or zig-zag undulations, should be especially avoided.

3. Where short curves occur, the walk should be hidden except immediately before the spectator; otherwise the increased distance may appear tiresome.

4. Walks running nearly parallel should be entirely hidden from each other.

5. They should have some definite object to reach, as a summer-house, arbor, or interesting point of view. "A walk that leads nowhere," says a late writer, "or ends in nothing, is always unsatisfactory."

6. Planting should be dense along such parts of the walk as require the concealment of unsightly objects, and open whenever fine prospects may be brought into view.

♦ ♦ ♦ ♦ ♦

When the soil has not been excavated, where the walk is made, to the depth of ten or twelve inches, and the excavation is not filled with stone, gravel, old mortar and other substances, the grass roots on each side of such walks will frequently run into the soil in the walk, and send up shoots so numerous that the walk will be quite green.

Make a weak brine and sprinkle the walks, by means of a water sprinkler, as often as the grass appears. A few pounds of salt used in this way will save a vast amount of hard hoeing, and, at the same time, keep such walks clean and neat.

Where there are quack roots, Canada thistle roots, or roots of any other noxious plants, it will be quite as well to sow the salt along the walks as it would to use brine.

Advice to Keep in View

Twenty years ago, I planted a clump of evergreens, mostly Norway spruces and hemlocks, to hide a neighbor's barn across the way. They have grown wondrously, and more than accomplished their object, for they have hidden a glimpse of a sheet of water that lies at the foot of a hill a mile away. The trees are too beautiful to be cut away, it would be sacrilege to trim them, and I am in a quandary to know what to do with them. In tree planting, one needs to look ahead a little, and see what a tree will become when it is well developed. Smaller evergreens would have hidden my eyesore, and saved my lake.

This may seem to be a small matter to people without taste, but it has a good deal to do with the happiness of the family. We ride miles to get a pretty view from the summit of a hill, and enjoy the whitening sails of the sea, or the steamers that leave behind them their long trails of smoke. Such a view, or any other pleasing prospect, would seem to be worth preserving at home. I am a little old-fashioned in my tastes, but really, I prefer to have these pictures out of doors, rather than their imitations upon the walls of the parlor.

From an 1863 issue of THE AMERICAN AGRICULTURIST

Removing Rocks

Dig by the side of the rock a hole large enough and deep enough to receive the stone and put it below the plow. When you have dug to the lower side of the rock, place a prop against it and the bank so as to hold it firm, and then dig under it a short distance to ascertain its size; then spade the hole to receive it. When all is ready take out the tools and pull out the prop, and if the rock does not drop a pry on the opposite side will soon drop it; then cover it over. It requires much less hard work to let a rock down than to raise it out of its bed, and the labor of drawing it away is a cleare gain. The thing is out of the way, and an eye-sore no longer.

From The Rural New Yorker, 1860

Have a Small Lawn

It is a mistaken notion that a lawn should be large. If of great extent, it lacks simplicity and home-likeness. It should be a cozy nook rather than a broad, open expanse. A large extent of surface is expensive to make and keep, and can hardly be maintained in that perfect order which is one of the great charms of a lawn. It should be large enough to show a few fine trees to advantage—their masses of foliage floating in the air, and their shadows stretching across the velvet turf; large enough for a wavy belt of shrubs on its borders, and running out, here and there, into the grass; large emough for children to romp and roll over it; but not large enough for a grove of trees to be planted upon it, nor for the review of a regiment of soldiers. It should be just large enough for the owner to keep it entirely free from weeds, its grass smooothly shaven and rolled, and its walks and flower-beds (if it contain them) in complete order.

From The Horticulturist Magazine, 1865

Simple Improvements

From The American Agriculturist, 1864

A pleasant home should never have an unpleasant approach. In the general spring clearing up, do not forget to put the door yard "to rights." We do not advocate anything stiff, formal, or expensive. Straighten up and repair the fence. Remove everything from the yard that does not belong there. Have a good walk from the gate to the front door, not one that is sunken below the general level and always flooded in rains; but let it be a little raised so as to be passable in all weathers. Have some flower borders by all means, but if there is unfortunately neither time nor taste for these, have grass and some trees and shrubs, not set in stiff rows, but dotted here and there. Then get a Virginia creeper (American Woodbine), or Wax

work vine from the woods and run it over the porch, if there is one, or if not, run it upon the door. A climbing rose may be easily obtained and will be very beautiful when in bloom. A small amount of work, and a little taste will make even a humble house look attractive and homelike.

Vines at the Door

From The American Agriculturist, 1877

If home-makers look after no other portion of the gardening, they are quite sure to take an interest in the vines, which cluster so closely around the door and windows, that they seem a part of the house rather than of the garden. Here is a common ground on which all can meet — the decoration of the house, for there is no work of the architect, however costly, but seems to need the final finish of vines, and no house, however poor in its exterior, but may be made to look home-like by the use of climbers. In our climate every house should have a veranda of some sort, even if but a mere porch, to shelter the door, and whether it be an extended veranda or narrow "stoop," there is a place for vines. The utility of vines, whether on the score of shade, or that of mere ornament, needs no showing, as all will admit it, and it becomes merely a question of ways and means — what to plant, and how to get it. Let us also say that if there is neither veranda or porch, and most log houses, and some houses of more pretentions have neither, one need not be without vines. A trellis of poles of some kind can be arranged to support the vines, and if it can be made of cedar and permanent, all the better, but if this can not be commanded, draw upon the stock of bean-poles, or get poles by some means that will answer for a season. No matter if it looks rude at first, the vines will charitably cover any sins of construction.

Don't Over·Do It

From The Horticulturist Magazine, 1865

Landscape gardening in a door-yard often verges upon the ridiculous. The proprietor, having read the standard authors, or visited a few large country residences, is seized with the rural fever, and determines to try his hand at improving his own place. He forthwith draws up a plan, with its winding walks and roads, its summer-houses, pines, oaks, magnolias, flower-patches, and what not. Large package of trees and shrubs and vines are ordered from the nursery, and groups and masses and screens are set out all in a grand way. The work looks very fine to the owner; but to any discerning eye that stops to forecast the future, the little plat looks crowded and overburdened before it is half planted. A few years roll by, and how does the place look to everybody? It is one great confused mass of foliage, the trees overgrowing each other, and killing out the grass and shrubs beneath. Even the planter himself is dissatisfied, and wishes he had never meddled with landscape gardening.

The obvious lesson from cases like this is that in small places only a few trees should be planted. These should be set along the boundaries, near the gates, and at wide intervals over the surface. Calculate their spread for twenty years or more to come, and plant accordingly. It is often said, we are aware, the trees may be set close together at first for immediate effect, with the design of removing a portion of them when they become crowded. This is all very well if that intention is faithfully carried out; but in most cases it is not. The owner dislikes to cut down the trees which he has planted, or he neglects to do so until they have grown up tall and gaunt, like those of a forest.

◆ ◆ ◆

Some beginners dot their lawn over with new-fangled trees, or crowd it with vases and statuary, or arbors, rustic seats and rock-work, or they throw it into jolting terraces, or cut it up into flower-beds in arabesque patterns. I remember a lawn of moderate dimensions in which there are six cast iron vases, two lions, four dogs, four female figures representing the Seasons, besides several other works in terra-cotta. This is the classical run mad. On the same street is another lawn, much smaller, in which a great number of the new weeping trees are huddled together. This is nature made awry, and the distortion makes the beholder uncomfortable. A single specimen of these oddities may sometimes be set on the side of a lawn, for variety, and just to show what nature and art can do, but more than one is too many.

◆ ◆ ◆

If landscape gardeners would always bear in mind that generally the simplest airs have the richest harmonies, that simplest subjects make the grandest pictures, and simplest designs make the most pleasing pleasure grounds, we would not be offended by so many strained, formal and unnatural garden effects. If they would use simpler lines and curves, and pay greater attention to fixing the places for permanent trees, they would produce much more charming effects. In small pleasure grounds avoid straight lines, in kitchen gardens avoid curves.

How to Establish a New Lawn

The soil should be made deep at the outset. If the land is poor, a coat of old manure should be turned under. This will prevent the drying up and burning out of the grasses in mid-summer, as it will cause the roots to strike deep for nourishment, and will furnish them the food they need. After the plowing, harrow smooth, sow the seed, brush it in, and afterward roll it. Cultivators are not perfectly agreed as to the best grasses for lawns. Some advise the sowing of only one kind of seed; others favor several. In some of the finest bits of natural lawn which we have noticed by the road-side, we have counted several sorts. Kentucky Blue Grass is a favorite in some quarters; other prefer Red Top. In the writer's experience both have done well; the Red Top was mixed with a little sweet scented vernal grass and white clover.

We have seen many a new lawn injured by too early cutting. To stand well, grass needs time to form large, vigorous roots, and to strike them well into the earth, but this they can not do if the tops are cut off. All that is taken from the top is so much lost to the roots. In the second and following years, when the roots become strong and well established, the mowing may be frequent.

From an 1863 issue of The American Agriculturist

Figure 1 — a badly trimmed hedge

How to
Plant and Grow a Perfect Hedge

From The American Agriculturist, 1879

♦ ♦ ♦ ♦ ♦

A perfect hedge is seldom seen in this country. Our people are in too much haste to see results, too impatient of the needful labor and cost, to build up a good, durable hedge, one that will turn cattle, and be a real ornament to any farm or residence. Consider, a moment, the conditions of such hedge building. The line must not run beneath the drip and shade of trees, or among their roots. The land must be good, or be made fertile by manure. The plants should be properly set out, the ground tilled and kept free of weeds for several years. And yet, how few enrich and cultivate soil along their hedge-rows, after the first year! Equal in importance to this, is thorough and systematic pruning every year. The majority of hedges are allowed to grow up several feet before they feel the shears at all. Of course, they become lank and bare at the bottom, where they ought to be bushy and strong. They are shaped more like the letter V, and must always remain so, while they ought to be more like that letter inverted. They should, from the start, be cut back every Spring to a foot of the new growth: i.e., the hedge should be allowed to gain in

Figure 2 — A properly trimmed hedge

height only one foot each year. The sides should be slightly trimmed, by all means keeping the lower branches broader than those above. The pruner should always keep in mind what the final shape of the hedge is to be. The inverted Λ seems to us a little too sharp, and we should advise rounding the sides a little, making it resemble a straw bee-hive, or rounded cone.

After the hedge is brought to its required height, say of four to six feet, it must be pruned at least once in mid-summer, to check its growth. Now, there are only a few persons who will take all this trouble, and this is a sufficient reason why we see so few good hedges.

Figure 3 — a neglected hedge

Privet Hedges

No one who has ever seen a rightly trimmed hedge of Privet can have failed to perceive what an important element in the furnishing of a lawn it makes. It adds as much to the effect of all the decorative planting as a frame does to a handsome picture. It is not browsed by cattle, even where fully exposed. It grows thick enough at the base to stop the smallest dog, pig, or fowl; it is nearly evergreen, and of a dark rich green, excellent as a backround for other shrubbery or for flowering plants. Its natural growth is erect, firm and hedge-like; it is very enduring, very rarely does a shoot die, and if that occurs others spring up freely. It is the easiest of propagation and easiest to trim, growing from cuttings very readily. South of Philadelphia the California Privet is as hardy as the common Privet is in the north. It has larger leaves, of a lighter green, very bright and glossy.

From Vick's Monthly Magazine, 1884

How to Plant Flower Seeds

From The Register of Rural Affairs, 1873

The rule which we have adopted for beds in open ground is to cover all seed from three to five times their shorter diameter — small seed receiving only a slight sprinkling, and larger a more copious sifting of the fine mould. No seed should be sown when the soil is not dry enough to be reduced to fine powder. The best soil is sandy loam, but a larger proportion of clay makes a good material if dry enough to be made perfectly mellow. The addition of sand and leaf-mould will make any soil of proper consistency. The best way to sow seeds is, in the first place, in drills or circles; then the weeds may be easily taken out. If sown broadcast, it will be more difficult to keep the bed clean. Provide a quantity of finely pulverized mould in a basket or barrow, and cover them by sprinkling it evenly over with the hand. Avoid soaking the beds with water until the plants are up. If the surface is likely to become too dry after sowing, which is often the case, put on a thin gauzy mulching. This may be pulverized moss, thin canvas, or even a newspaper.

A Garden Seat

From the August, 1864 issue of The American Agriculturist

Here is an ingenious contrivance, to save the strain of the backs, and muscles of the legs of persons whose labors require them to maintain a stooping posture, when they have frequently to move short distances, and hence can not take an ordinary stool with them. Especially is this adapted to relieve the nurserymen and gardeners in some of their labors——for instance in grafting and budding near the ground; weeding; and setting out plants with which considerable pains have to be taken. The construction is easily seen by the engraving. A metal sole is firmly attached to the foot; upon this sole and just back of the heel is a socket into which fits a straight ash stick of convenient length, and upon the top of this is a circular disk of wood which affords a very comfortable support to the body, taking the greater part of the weight entirely off the legs. The user walks with the seat attached to his foot. It is not in the way of any common movements, and instead of being a temptation to indolence, is rather an inducement for a gardner to stick to his work, and not find an excuse to get up and walk off somewhere to ease his legs.

Door Yard Hints

Flowering shrubs and those with brilliantly colored foliage are to ornamental gardening what the finishing touches are to the picture or the varnishing is to furniture. They help to fill out the well-rounded forms of groups of trees and, possessing more variety of colors of flowers and foliage than the large trees, they add beautiful bits of color to often otherwise tame garden-work. Being small in size, they are especially useful in planting places of small extent, are comparatively inexpensive, and reach maturity in a very short time. They are very useful in ornamenting the foreground where it is desired to take in views above and beyond the limits of small grounds, and serve the purpose of a setting or ornamentation close up to the dwelling and over which may be viewed the more extended lawn decoration.

From the 1899 book, Landscape Gardening

◆ ◆ ◆

Can we say anything to induce land-owners to keep their grounds cleaner? It has been justly remarked that we are a weedy nation, and if the weeds annually raised within our boundaries were clover and wheat instead, they would amount to sixty million dollars. Probably this is too low an estimate. We are glad to observe that there is a distinct improvement in this respect, both in gardens and on farms, within a few years, throughout the country. But it is hard to make some men understand that if they can kill or eradicate half the weeds, there is no reason why they cannot root out the other half. We have been trying to teach this doctrine to one of our hired men, who seems to entertain conscientious scruples against making a clean sweep of the weeds. He seems resolved to leave at least a tenth of the whole amount, and we cannot make him understand that if the first tenth may be killed, the last tenth may be also. We once visited a nurseryman who occupied thirty-five acres, but who kept no weeds! "How do you manage to kill all the weeds?" was our question. "We do not kill them—we never allow them an entrance."

From The Register of Rural Affairs, 1874

◆ ◆ ◆

Amateurs who desire to increase their favorite shrubs, Roses or vines, will find layering the best method, and July the best month, to perform the operation. Although too slow a process for nurserymen who desire to multiply their stock rapidly, it is far the best method for all who require a few extra plants. Select the north side of the plant to lay down the branch to be rooted, and pulverize the soil well where the new plant is to take root.

From an 1885 issue of Vick's Monthly Magazine

If perennials are selected among the hardier and stronger sorts, they will maintain their appearance and thriftiness with a small amount of cultivation — no more than shrubs commonly require for their successful growth.

From The Register of Rural Affairs, 1877

In order to prolong the flowering season in perpetual and other roses, and in annual and perennial plants, clip off with a pair of scissors the seed-vessels, as soon as the petals fall. This prevents the exhaustion of the plant in the forming of seed, continues its vigor, and preserves a neater appearance of the whole plant. At the same time, the use of the scissors will enable the gardener to impart a symmetrical form to the plants.

From The Register of Rural Affairs, 1865

Vines

Among the best results of nature's effort to cover and beautify the waste places of earth, the luxurious growth of climbing vines and creepers is not the least. Were we to remove all of this class of plants from the forests and ravines of our land, there would be a stiffness in the landscape and a barrenness where beauty now prevails. We should also lose much of the verdure of the summer and nearly all of the rich high-coloring of the autumn foliage.

This suggests that there are places which would be improved in appearance by judicious plantings of some of the most desirable of the many climbing plants, so near by us that they would need but little care, except proper planting.

Probably the most unsightly places are where the sloping banks are left uncared for, at the sides of our streets and roadways, as grading and cutting away banks is done in ordinary improvements. The sloping side of a bank will be left to the action of water and frost, so that deep cuts will appear; the soil is barren and is easily washed into gutters to their injury, or to cave in and destroy the surface above, and often undermine and ruin fine specimens of trees or foundations of buildings.

The wasting of these banks can be prevented by planting thickly on their sides such climbing plants as Virginia Creeper, (Ameplopsis quinquefolia,) Bitter Sweet, (Honeysuckles of strong growing varieties,) Dutchman's Pipe, (Aristolochia sipho,) Trumpet Vine, (Tecoma,) native Clematis and Wistarias. All these plants thrive well in any soil. They root easily as they spread, and take such a firm hold of the banks that the washing away is prevented; so the utility of the plan is exceeded only by the beauty of the mixed greens in the foliage, and the changes of scarlet which follow the colors of blossoms and fruit.

Most of the plants I have mentioned are also suitable for covering barren or rocky places, if a crevice can be found by the roots. Unsightly mounds, old stumps and tree trunks can be made beautiful by very little care, and at slight, if any, cost.

◆ ◆ ◆

The use of climbing vines is general for verandas and trellises to serve for screens and shade. As there is a large variety to select from for planting, so there is much diversity as to places of planting. Where large surfaces are to be covered only the strongest growing varieties should be chosen; probably the best for this is the Virginia Creeper, but the blossoms on this are not conspicuous, so it may be desirable to train on the same trellis a few fine-blooming plants for blossom and fragrance, like Clematis, Honeysickle or Tecoma.

Where the top of a porch or screen is not over ten feet, there is a large list of plants to select from; notably Clematis, both native and hybrids, of glorious beauty and marvelous bloom, embracing nearly all colors and seasons. The Clematis requires a good soil, rich and deep, and the planting should not be made too close to buildings or cellars, as nothing should interfere with natural moisture or sunlight.

We must not overlook the Ampelopsis veitchii (Japan or Boston Ivy), as it will climb, of itself, up and along stone or brick walls, and, without care, cover the whole side of very large buildings. It is a matter of interest that this plant was brought to this country about thirty years ago, and was then regarded as a delicate little climber, suitable only for hanging baskets in the conservatory; but to-day there are countless thousands produced annually, and it is known to this generation as a hardy and rugged plant, and speaks for itself from the walls of the finest residences and churches, outstripping in beauty all the architect can boast of.

From the Annual Report of the New York State Agricultural Society, 1896

Flower Garden Hints

The grass of borders and lawns must be kept closely cut, the flower-beds carefully weeded, and the flowers watered at night if the weather is dry.

Night is the best time for watering. The plants are then thirsty, having been exposed all day to the heat of the sun; the ground dry and warm from the same cause, and a plentiful supply of cold water reduces the temperature and revives the plant. There is all the night for the water to penetrate the ground and moisten the soil around the roots. If watered in the morning, the plants are already cool, and the cold water might reduce their temperature too low. Then the heat of the sun coming so soon to evaporate the moisture, the water has not the same time it has at night to do service to the plants.

The annuals have by this time attained such a height, that the more slender ones will require some support. Tie them to sticks, letting their foliage conceal the stocks as much as possible. Dahlias will now also need to be staked. Strings and poles must be provided for vines if it is not already done.

Cuttings of blossoms can now be taken with perfect safety, and the more frequently the plants are cut, the longer and more profuse will be their bloom. Some plants, such as candytuft and sweet alyssum, require constant cutting to keep a succession of bloom through the season.

Flowers are beautiful additions for the breakfast or dinner table. A bouquet by each plate is a pretty conceit, and a centre-piece of flowers may be made really exquisite in appearance. It is not necessary to have a complete supply of china or silver ware to find a proper stand for your flowers. Always remembering that it is the flowers themselves, not their receptacle, which is destined to ornament the table.

From the July, 1870 issue of Arthur's Home Magazine.

If those who have had little experience with plants, look over the catalogues and make their selections from the descriptions there given, they will very often be disappointed. Flowers must have certain requisites to make them popular, and mere novelty will never satisfy the great mass of cultivators. The fact is that for people in general, not one fourth of the flowers of the seed lists are worth growing — not because they are not good of their kind, but because they are not of a kind which meets the popular idea of a flower. To be satisfactory, an annual must be a free bloomer, and last a long while in bloom; the flowers must be showy individually, or in the mass, and be of good color, or to compensate for a lack of these qualities, they must have a pleasing fragrance. A plant with a tall weedy growth, with here and there a showy flower of short duration, may be interesting and pretty, but will never be popular.

From The American Agriculturist, 1864

Plant a Wild Garden

◆ ◆ ◆ ◆ ◆

The Wild Garden is a place where interesting wild and cultivated plants are brought together in the most natural manner, and allowed to live and struggle, much as they do when wild. In small grounds a place in the midst of groups of trees and shrubs, or in large grounds a number of acres partly wood and partly open, treated thus for revealing the wildness peculiar to woods and clearings, may be rendered a most enjoyable place. Where space will admit, hardy flowers, grasses, ferns, and creepers should be scattered about, and thickets be formed of shrubs, including brambles. Some clumps of the more graceful wild-looking plants of the garden should be placed here, together with those gathered from woods and clearings. Some annuals may be scattered over the soil in spots, to come along as they can, and some of these will live for years by self-seeding.

From the 1893 book, ORNAMENTAL GARDENING FOR AMERICANS

Make Your Own
Wildflower Mix

Most 19th Century seed catalogs listed a "wildflower" mix for easy maintenance in door yard gardens. By sowing Mignonette, Candytuft, Larkspurs, Marigolds, Poppies, Foxgloves and other hardy seeds together in borders, yesterday's landscapers could almost duplicate the beauty of nature's gardens and could be sure of a constant succession of color.

Try it yourself or add a small amount of the same mixture to decorative grass seed for a beautiful "wild" meadow. — D.J.B.

Hints on Growing Roses

More people appreciate the beauty and value of the rose than that of any other flower, but comparatively few succeed in growing it to its greatest perfection. It succeeds best in a deep rich soil, rather moist and of somewhat a clayey nature. More persons fail in growing the rose from not making the soil rich enough than from any other cause.

Perhaps the best line of treatment is to spade the bed 18 to 24 inches deep, working in fine rotted cow manure and leaf mould to the full depth, and every fall banking up against each plant a foot or more with rich stable manure for protection. In the spring this manure should be spread on the surface of the bed and spaded in, and if the soil is not too thin and dry a good growth and an abundance of blossoms will result.

In pruning the work may be done either in the fall or in March, the latter time being generally preferred. In this work the bushes should be so pruned as to obtain a limited number of as strong canes as possible. The stronger the canes the larger will be the flowers. All weak shoots should be either severely cut back or entirely removed and the strong canes headed back one half or two thirds, varying the treatment somewhat with the variety and the size and number of flowers required; some varieties, especially the very strong growing ones, needing less pruning than others, but with all varieties the smaller the number of shoots the larger will be the flowers. For winter protection, banking up against the collar of the bushes a foot or more with soil or manure should be practised with all outdoor roses, and most of them will be much benefited by tying up in coarse rye-straw or mats. Pine boughs set up closely about them for the winter will improve the quality of the blossoms very greatly.

From the 1899 book, Landscape Gardening

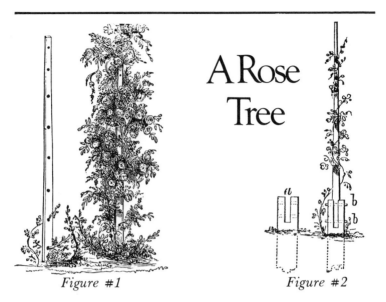

A Rose Tree

Figure #1 Figure #2

Would you like to display your climbing roses at their best? A cedar board with 2" holes drilled at 1' intervals becomes the support for a "rose tree," a standard in yesterday's garden. Plant two varieties of roses, for a mix of color and pass the leading shoots of each through the same hole, from opposite directions. Intertwine and train the climbers as they grow and you'll soon have, in the words of J.J. Thomas "a most brilliant exhibition," as shown in Figure #1 above. The illustrations are from Thomas' 1855 book, *RURAL AFFAIRS*.

Tender roses can be rested on the ground and covered in winter if the rose tree is simply supported from a post with two horizontal pins, as shown in Figures #2 and #3. Remove the top pin and the lower one becomes a hinge. The best protection for the plants is a light covering of evergreen boughs. They'll insulate the roses from cold winds and still look good in the winter landscape.

For best effect, plant your rose tree near a background of evergreens or dense foliage. Rose trees set a foot or so away from a foundation become a beautiful decoration for barren walls and plain screened porches. — DJB

Figure #3

A Simple Safe Insect Powder

I have been in the habit of using, for three years or more, a mixture, first made known to me by a German farmer, that I am much pleased with. In almost every case in which I have applied it, success has followed its application; and the insects have been driven away, and the plants preserved.

The mixture is a very simple one. Take some dry ground plaster of Paris, spread it, and sprinkle over it, from a bottle, spirits of turpentine—turning over the plaster so as to slightly moisten the whole. Let it dry, and then rub it or pound it slightly till it is quite fine again.

Now it is ready for use; and to use it, you have only to scatter it over the leaves or stems of plants liable to be infested or attacked by insects. In order to have it adhere to the foliage, it is best to use it early in the morning, while the leaves are wet with dew.

I have found it effectually to protect melons and cucumbers from the striped bug, grape-vines from the small white fly, and even drive away the rose bug from such plants as it was applied to.

From The Horticulturist Magazine, 1848

Figure 1   *Figure 2*

Bird Houses

◆ ◆ ◆ ◆ ◆

From The American Agriculturist, 1864

Birds are a joy about any house. Blithe, cheerful, musical, industrious, they impart of their pleasant tempers to the air almost, and make the garden and all their haunts lively with happy animation. Their use to the farmer and gardener has often been commented upon. They are indeed almost the only effective check to the increase of many species of destructive insects, and must be regarded by all tillers of the soil as most valuable collaborators. Those birds, which naturally build their nests in holes, take up their dwelling in bird houses very readily, if these be provided.

Fig. *1* is a single bluebird house, very easily constructed, which may be nailed upon a tree or building.

Fig. *2* is a wren house, 3½ or 4 inches by 5, made also for nailing up. The number of these little busy wrens one may collect about his place by putting up a large number of these houses, is surprising. Two pairs will not use the same house, even if there are several holes. They quarrel with bluebirds and will drive them away, hence it is best to keep them in different parts of the grounds. If wrens have a very small house they will soon fill it with sticks and make a nest; but if the house is large, it sometimes seems as they did nothing else all summer but fill it with twigs, and tear them out again. So the best way is to give the fidgety little fellows small quarters, that they may devote all their spare time to the insects.

A Play House

Let your kids have a play house this summer, Find a shady, out of the way spot in your yard and follow the old-time formula: give your children some scrap lumber, tools and nails and then leave them alone. You might want to supervise the basic structure — a frame of 2"x6"s nailed securely to some low tree limbs or a platform built on solid fence posts, but besides that, and checking for exposed nail points, let them build it. They'll spend countless hours planning, building and altering. They'll be exercising their bodies and their minds. In the end they'll have something that they can truly call their own.

If their creation doesn't meet your architectural standards, it's a fault of your imagination. The illustration is of the play house of an 1876 estate — a mansion with acres of carefully cultivated gardens whose owner hadn't forgotten his childhood. Did you have a tree house or a quiet spot carved out of an overgrown hedge when you were young? How does that memory look now? – DJB

Plant for Profit

♦ ♦ ♦ ♦ ♦

Instances could be multiplied to show that, for from two to five per cent of the value of a place, spent on garden improvements, returns of from ten to sixty per cent in increased value have been realized in a short time. Trees, shrubs, climbers, and plants in choice kinds, well arranged, develop rapidly and greatly increase the valuation of a place, through angmenting the beauty of the architecture and the general effect. The presence of these always makes a less expensive house look finer than a costlier one, which presents nothing in the heat of summer, or in the storms of winter, for the eye to rest upon, but bare walls and harsh outlines, unbroken by any trees or other vegetation.

Many a man with the means and disposition, will pay several thousand dollars to architect, builder, and furnisher, for a house, with the view that the beauty and comfort purchased will yield satisfaction proportionate to the cost. To such a person it may be said, that one thousand dollars prudently invested in arranging and planting the home grounds, may be made to pay a much larger percentage of pure pleasure and interest, than the same amount put into the building. If one who is about investing five thousand dollars, or a smaller or larger amount, in improving a home, should keep back five per cent of the sum and invest it in improving the surroundings, it may be made to yield far better returns in the years to come, than if nearly all had been spent on the house, and a mere pittance allowed for the grounds.

Will it pay to plant trees on the average farm? A view, such as may be sometimes had, of two farms, of the same size and general situation, but presenting strong contrasts in the presence and absence of trees and shrubs respectively, may throw light on the question. One of the farms may have half a dozen large shade trees about the yard, some climbers over the piazzas and building; dense clumps of evergreens, both for beauty and to serve as wind-breaks. It may also have a number of broad shade trees in the barn-yard, along the lanes, the boundaries, creeks, and in other places where nothing else can be profitably grown, yielding grateful shade and shelter. The other has not a sign of sylvan beauty, with every part without shelter by trees from the summer's sun or the winter's gales. The trees on the first farm may have cost one hundred dollars for stock, setting, etc., while any disinterested person would estimate the value they add to the place, at ten-fold greater than their cost.

No better method can be devised for rendering farming a pleasant occupation to the young, than the judicious use of trees and garden beauty about the grounds. Our attachments to trees becomes almost as strong as to persons, and if there are fine ones growing about the home, and with them some good shrubs, climbers, flowers, etc., they will add new strength to the chain which binds the heart of youth to the hearthstone, and to the rural pursuits among which they have been reared.

From the book, ORNAMENTAL GARDENING FOR AMERICANS, 1893

♦ ♦ ♦ ♦ ♦

THE
DOOR YARD
CALENDAR

From 1862 thru 1884 issues of
The American Agriculturist

January

CHRISTMAS GREENS, when taken down are very handy to give a little additional protection wherever needed.

EVERGREENS are apt to be bent out of shape, by accumulation of snow in their tops. It should be shaken out while light; in snows heavy enough to cover their lower branches, shovel away and clear them, or they may be broken as the snow hardens and settles. Small evergreens of untested kinds, should have spruce or other evergreen boughs placed around them for a few winters.

LAWNS should be raked, to gather up all litter, and then rolled to settle the soil. A top-dressing of fine compost spread upon it will induce a healthy and thrifty growth. Seed thin spots.

PLANTS in cellars and frames should be aired when the weather will allow. Do not water unless they are very dry.

PLANTING.—Make preparations for planting early. Mark the position each tree and shrub is to occupy upon a plan, so that no time will be lost in consultation when the ground is dry enough to work.

PRUNING TREES AND SHRUBS should be done only when necessary. If shrubs are pruned, observe the natural habit of each, and do not expect to make one with curving branches grow erect. It is the variety of form quite as much as variety of color, that gives beauty to a clump of shrubs. Never disfigure an evergreen by cutting away its lower branches.

RUSTIC WORK is an important embellishment in the surroundings of a house. There are many climbing plants well adapted to rustic trellises and arbors, and rustic flower-boxes placed here and there upon the lawn for ornamental plants add much to the beauty of a place. A little taste in the selection of materials and skill in making up these rustic ornaments are all that is needed; Laurel and Cedar are the woods most used for this purpose.

STAKES AND LABELS.—Prepare a good supply of these for use in the spring. Give all a coating of paint, for convenience in reading the names when written. If the ends which are to be placed in the ground are soaked in petroleum they will last much longer.

February

Unless the weather is mild enough to admit of transplanting, but little work can be done in the grounds. Still they should be watched to see that any damage from winds or snow be avoided or remedied. The borders present a dreary appearance at this season. Recollect in the planting season to provide against this, especially if they are where they are visible from the house. The borders may be made to wear a cheerful look, even in Winter, by a judicious introduction of evergreen shrubbery, the foliage of which will set off the flowers in Summer, and be pleasant to look upon in Winter. The Holly-leaved Barberry, Rhododendrons, Tree Box, Laurel, Daphne Cneorum, and others, according the locality, may be used. Make all projected improvements on paper.

PROTECTION.—Inexperienced persons are apt to remove this as soon as they think the severity of winter has passed. Many things require protection, not on account of the severe cold of our climate, but from the sudden alternations of heat and cold in Spring. If the straw or other covering has been torn off by the wind, have it replaced. A warm spell this month may induce some things to start too early. Shade these from the sun.

SHRUBBERY.—Have an eye to it after a heavy fall of snow. In mild weather pruning may be done. Pruning does not mean an indiscriminate cutting at a bush. Those shrubs which flower on the new wood, should be cut in a way to induce a vigorous new growth. Many flower only on the wood of the previous year, and should be only sparingly thinned when the branches are too crowded.

TRANSPLANT shrubs and deciduous trees whenever the ground is in suitable condition for working. Determine beforehand, what the effect will be, before you plant out or remove a tree or shrub.

TRELLISES.—Repair old and make new ones. If disposed to try your hand at ornamental work, choose simple and graceful forms rather than elaborate ones. Study what the effect will be when covered with vines.

WHAT MAY BE DONE?—Stone may be got out and hauled into heaps where it may be wanted for sale or for use. A well may be dug in the barn yard. Posts and rails may be got out in the rough hauled to a convenient spot, and piled up to dry. Slabs from a saw-mill make excellent fence posts, and can usually be purchased very cheaply, and these may be drawn home. Springs may be cleaned out and walled up. Rocks may be undermined and toppled into large holes and buried. To a willing worker, there never comes a time when there is nothing to be done; and much may be done now to prepare for the busier period which will soon be at hand.

March

Many of the things indicated last month will lap over into the present one. If the grass of the lawn did not have a top-dressing in autumn, put on one of rich compost, early in the season, and reseed thin places. Happy is he who last fall planted generously of bulbs, for he now is rewarded by a sight of the green spires of the Crocus, and the Snow-drop and Hyacinth are full of promise, if not present enjoyment.

FLOWERING SHRUBS of all the hardy kinds, roses included, do best if planted early, but roses that have been started in pots, must not be put out yet. The number of flowering shrubs is so large that we must refer to the catalogues for names. For early flowering, Forsythia, Wiegelas, Japan Quince, and the finer lilacs are all readily procurable.

HARDY ANNUALS, such as Candy-Tuft, Larkspur, and all that are known to come readily from self-sown seeds, may be sown as early as the frost will allow.

HARDY CLIMBERS have claims which ought not to be overlooked. The Virginia Creeper, Trumpet Creeper, Wistaria, the Honeysuckles, Climbing roses and many others will cover an unsightly wall with a mantle of beauty.

NEW LAWNS should be made as early as the ground is in good condition, to have the grass well established before hot weather. For light soils, Red-top, for stony ones, Blue-grass, with perhaps a little White Clover, is in our experience preferable to mixed seeds. Four to six bushels to the acre are needed to make a good velvety turf.

OLD LAWNS will need a top-dressing and a sprinkling of seed in places where the grass is poor. If manure is applied, let it be so thoroughly decomposed that no weed-seeds remain alive. Ashes, guano, nitrate of soda and fine bone, are all good manures for lawns and bring in no weeds.

TREES for the lawn, yard, and roadside, should receive the same care in the selection of specimens, careful planting and soil, that is given to fruit trees. A tree is very difficult to kill, but many who set them out for ornament, very nearly succeed in doing it. If wild trees are used, select them from the edges of the woods and exposed situations, and choose those of moderate size.

April

The love of flowers is as natural to a man as is his breath— but alas! the love of profit that may be counted in dollars and cents, leads too many to overlook the enjoyment which springs from so much purer and higher a source. A little taste and care, with a very little expense of time or money, will make the surroundings of the humblest cottage most attractive and beautiful; and the wealth of the Indies may be lavished for years upon glass houses and gardens, and still we shall have but just begun to see with what varied, delicate and gorgeous beauty of the floral world, nature will reward our care. Every one may have flowers.

Before laying out a new place, provide for a liberal garden spot, give it a warm sunny aspect, some shaded nooks, a good, well drained soil, and allow it a good share of manure. The soil must be well worked, mellow and free from weeds —But some nice flowers grow anywhere.

FLOWERING SHRUBS—Plant the althea, flowering almond, azalea, chionanthus, flowering currant, deutzia, euonymus, holly, Japan quince, laburnum, lilac, philadelphus, rose acacia, snowberry, snowball, spiraea, tree poeony, weigelia, etc. Early flowering shrubs give a finer bloom if transplanted as soon as ground is in working order.

GRAVEL WALKS—Add gravel to old and new walks as needed. Clean out any weeds or grass, cover with gravel, rake smoothly, and press down with heavy roller.

HEDGES—Set out privet, althaea, buckthorn, Arbor Vitae, etc., for hedges. Osage Orange and honey locust are of too rampant and coarse a growth for handsome screens or protection around dwellings and pleasure grounds.

LABELS AND STAKES—Provide an ample supply.

LAWNS—Sow grass seed on thin spots, scarifying with a sharp rake, and roll. Top dress with guano water, or ammoniacal water from gas works, or with Chili saltpetre, ashes, plaster or superphosphate.

MANURE heavily all the borders and flowers plots.

EVERGREENS—Arbor Vitae and Norway Spruce may be transplanted freely at this season; others in May or June.

ROSES—The almost endless variety of monthly, remontant, and common sorts, enables the cultivater to secure a rich profusion and constant succession of bloom. Purchase and set out blooming plants, and such only as have a good reputation for hardiness and free blooming. The Romontant, sometimes called Hybrid Perpetual, will give good satisfaction. Plant out, prune and tie those trained to trellises or pillars.

SHADE TREES—Plant deciduous sorts early. Many of our choicest fruit trees are beautiful as shade trees, for instance, the bigarreau cherries, the crab apple, and pears growing uniform pyramids.

May

All re-arranging and laying out and transplanting of trees and shrubs is to be hurried as rapidly as possible.

BULBS.—The bloom of hyacinths or tulips can be prolonged by shading from hot sun by cloth awning.

BOX EDGING.—Clip the old and set new.

BEDDING PLANTS—Petunias, Verbenas, etc., may be put out.

CLIMBERS.—Seeds of the Cypress Vine and some newer Morning-glories germinate better if soaked 12 hours in warm water, or having water poured over as hot as the hand can bear.

EVERGREENS.—Plant upon the lawn and as screens. Broad-leaved evergreens should not be forgotten. Holly, Rhododendrons, Laurel, and the little Daphne Cneorum are among useful ones.

GRAVEL WALKS.—Keep in order with rake and roller.

HEDGES.—Complete setting the new and clip the old. Fill weak places by weaving in the branches.

HONEYSUCKLES and other woody climbers, plant

early. Put up and tie securely to trellises those removed for winter protection. Layer for increase.

LABELS AND STAKES.—Have a plenty at hand to mark every thing sown. Do not trust to memory. Dahlia stakes should be set out with the plant.

LANTANAS.—These do best in a rather sandy soil, with plenty of sun. They grow rapidly and may be pegged down as bedding plants, or trained to bush form, to be potted in autumn and kept over winter.

LAWNS.—Mow as soon as the grass will take the scythe.

MULCH.—All newly planted trees will be benefited by covering the earth around them with any thing which will prevent evaporation. Stable litter, straw, haulm of beans and peas, chips, tan-bark, or saw-dust may be used. Even the early mowings of the lawn may be profitably used in this manner.

LILIES.—The different species of these, even when planted in spring, make a fine show the same season. The different varieties of the Japan Lily are all beautiful; the bulbs are all perfectly hardy, and the flowers of all are finer than those of any other kinds. They should be in every garden, and will flourish in any good soil. The old White should not be forgotten, and our native sorts are improved by cultivation and are very showy.

MIGNONETTE.—This is grown for its perfume, as the flowers are not showy. A bed of this and Candytuft make a good mixture, as one furnishes the fragrance while the other supplies the show.

PETUNIAS.—These are among the most popular bedding plants. Good results may be had from seeds sown early, but the finer sorts can only be procured by cuttings in the green-house. The double varieties, if used as bedding plants, need much care, as their blooms are easily broken off.

ROSES.—These may still be planted. Do not forget the old fashioned June roses. The now popular Remontants and Bourbons have nearly driven these old favorites from the gardens. Turn the Teas from the pots into the open border. Keep climbers tied up. Remove layers made last season.

TREES AND SHRUBS.—Continue to plant if the work is not finished, and protect by tieing to stakes.

VERBENAS.—Plant in masses. If any have run up to flower, cut them back severely before planting.

WEEDS.—If there are any in the borders the garden is too large. Not a weed should be seen.

June

The earliest harvests of the year are gathered in the flower garden. The blossoming is to us fruition—and in June Nature's lap is full of flowers. Seed time still continues, many annuals may be sown. It is well to sow a little deeper than in May, and sometimes to lay a light board over the spot for a day or two, so as to keep the soil moist, but to remove it before the seeds begin to start much. Seeds of biennials may be sown at any time during this month or next, though with many kinds a tolerably long season, and vigorous growth the first season are essential to perfection of flowering the nest.

There may be much taste exercised in the location of annuals and bedding plants, so that as they come successively into bloom, the garden may not appear bright and bare in spots, nor get mixed up blue and white and red and yellow, like the old fashioned style of "splashing" book edges—but so that there shall be a profusion of flowers grouped in masses all over it. A mass of bloom need not be large, but only enough to destroy the awkward, lonely effect of single flowers or spikes of the same kind, looking up here and there all over a garden, but each by itself. This remark is not applicable to the more independent and robust flowers like foxgloves, balsams or Dahlias, which often are very effective quite alone.

BEDDING PLANTS should be set early this month, and kept in proper shape by pinching. Coleuses will often throw up flower-stalks during the summer, but these should be cut as soon as they show, else the effect of the bed is injured.

BULBS—Spring blooming bulbs when they have passed the flowering, should stand a while in the ground; then be lifted, with so much earth only as adheres to the roots and laid with their labels in empty flower pots under some cover where they will dry in the shade, and will not be wet by rains. When dry remove the tops, wrap in papers and keep dry until planting time in the Autumn.

CLIMBERS of all kinds should be kept within bounds, and under good training. Their appearance is greatly improved by very little time occasionally given to them.

EVERGREEN—June is emphatically the month to transplant evergreens with best success.

GRASS EDGINGS AND BORDERS—Keep closely cut and trimmed always. If it burns in spots or looks ragged, water with liquid manure, and sift on a quarter of an inch in depth of fine loam.

GRAVEL WALKS—First, plenty of gravel often raked; second, a good roller, often used; third, a shuffle hoe, to cut up weeds wherever they appear, are what will secure good walks. The weeds are left to dry and disappear on the surface, when not neglected, and grown too large.

HEDGES—Clip full grown hedges as often as they make growth enough. Evergreen hedges are best trimmed before they make their new growth. Young hedges must be pruned severely to force low branching. It is very easy to get top branches, but impossible to thicken up a neglected hedge near the ground, and such a hedge is neither ornamental nor useful.

INSECTS—Rose slugs, destroy with oil soap. The solution should be very dilute, and applied with a garden syringe and not a sprinkling water pot; they are on the underside of the leaves. This is also a defense against other insects.

WEEDS.—The hoe and rake and fingers must be kept in motion and the weeds have no quarter.

July

The main things to be done here are those which will secure neatness. After the abundance of spring flowers is over, many are apt to allow the garden and lawn to run into neglect. Weeds appear, plants which should be tied up are allowed their own way, unsightly flower stalks, from which the bloom has fallen, remain, and a general want of care is manifest such as no garden should present. With proper care, the attractions of the garden may be made to last until vegetation is stopped by frost.

As too frequently cultivated there is a dearth of flowers in July. Many of the early bedding and other plants, including the bulbs, lilies, paeonies, dicentra, roses, etc., are nearly out of flower, and it is too early for the annuals, and for dahlias, gladioluses and other Autumn bloomers. The chief reliance must now be upon the verbenas, petunias, fuchsias, heliotropes, pinks, geraniums, hollyhocks, tall phlox, salvias, some of the remontant roses, etc.

EVERGREENS.—Prune and do not let the upper branches overhang the lower ones.

GRAVEL WALKS.—Keep out weeds by use of the hoe and rake, and put fresh gravel on any thin spots.

GRASS.—The lawn should be mowed often and edges of paths and borders neatly trimmed. Grass used for edgings to beds needs the same care.

HEDGES.—Clip into shape and plash or weave in the branches to fill up weak places.

LAWN—The grass of the lawn should be mowed just as often as a sharp scythe will cut anything. If you have water supplied in pipes from a head, by all means have a hydrant situated so that with a hose the grass may be often sprinkled. If moss comes in, after scarifying with a rake, a sifting of soil ¼ inch deep over the spot and a sprinkling of wood ashes, with a little salt, on the surface will probably destroy it.

PERENNIALS.—If seed is not required, the flower-stalk should be cut when the bloom is over, to throw all the strength into the roots. Some tall kinds require stakes, to keep them in position. Use the rake and hoe often, to kill the young weeds; a steel-toothed rake does very effective work, if used when the weeds are small.

ROSES! ROSES—Is there a family in this wide land with a rod of land attached to their dwelling, that has not a rose bush? Roses grow wild in almost every country, and by cultivation the number of varieties is rendered almost infinits. So numerous are they that the Horticulturist shrinks from enumerating even a few of the best sorts. The country gardens blush with them, and city corners and market places are redolent with their perfume. Severe cutting back after the bloom has nearly past, will secure on many varieties, particularly such as ordinarily bloom twice in the season, a full bloom again much sooner and fuller than otherwise. If roses depended upon for fall bloom are cut back to the sacrifice of their flowers at this season, they will blossom much earlier and finer for it. Keep climbers from whipping about in the wind, by binding them to the pillars or trellises. Prune all roses as soon as they have flowered, letting no seed remain except on those varieties of cluster roses like the Sweet briar on which the clusters of coral-colored hips are so ornamental.

SEED STALKS—As soon as the flowers are past, remove the stalk, unless seed is wanted, in which case tie it up, or mark it in some way so that it shall not be disturbed. A heedless person in the garden may destroy some very choice seed if it be not protected in some such way.

VERBENAS need to be watched and pinned down so as to cover the whole bed allotted to them as speedily as possible. Ladies' hair-pins are excellent for this purpose. If the flower heads are all pinched off before they blossom it

PROPAGATION.—Many of the ornamental shrubs may be multiplied from cuttings of the new growth set in sandy soil in a shady place, and kept moist.

PRUNING.—If necessary to do this to lawn trees, the present is the favorable month.

RHODODENDRONS.—The hot weather of summer is often injurious to these. Insure moisture at the roots by properly mulching.

ROSES.—The new growth if layered now will form plants to be removed next spring. Cut back the perpetuals as soon as their first bloom is over. Keep the climbing and pillar roses well tied up. Apply a solution of whale oil soap, 1 pound to 6 or 8 gallons of water, if the rose slug appears.

SEEDS.—Save the finest flowers for seed. Collect as they ripen and label at once.

VERBENAS.—These and other bedding plants need pegging down. Layers and cuttings made now will root rapidly and give late flowering plants.

August

Keep the soil stirred this hot month; it will be found more beneficial than watering. Observe neatness, not only in in keeping ahead of weeds, but in tying up plants that need it, removing spent flower stalks and all unsightly matters. Mow the lawn and grass edgings at least once a week; let no coarse weeds get established. Give summer clipping to box edgings and deciduous hedges.

BULBS—Such as the hyacinth and tulip, should be lifted as soon as the leaves turn yellow, the offsetts removed, and the bulbs dried and put away in paper bags until Autumn, then re-planted. This has a tendency to keep them more vigorous and truer to their colors. If necessary to remove them before the foliage is ripened off well, take up a ball of earth with the bulb, and re-set until the foliage is ripened.

CLIMBERS.—Provide proper supports and see that they cling to them. They often need a little help.

HEDGES should receive their final Summer clipping during this month. Cut from the top. If cut late in the growing season, the new growth will not sufficiently mature before Winter.

HOEING.—During the dry season the hoe and rake must be kept in use, not only to remove weeds, but to loosen the soil and help sustain the plants.

INSECTS.—Though these are not as troublesome as in former months, there is still need of watchfulness. Dusting of lime or ashes, and syringing with oil soap will be needed. Above all, hand-picking is the great remedy. When an insect is caught and crushed he is sure to be of no further trouble.

LAYERS.—Almost everything in the way of woody plants, and the firmer herbaceous ones, can be multiplied by layers.

LAWN AND GRASS EDGINGS—Mow evenly as soon as 6 to 8 inches high. Frequent cutting causes it to thicken at the bottom. A sprinkling of guano water, or liquid manure, after cutting, will cause the grass to start with vigor. New lawns may be sown adding a little Winter wheat, or rye, to protect the roots during the Winter.

PERENNIALS.—A year may be saved by sowing the seed of most of them now. Fox-gloves, Sweet Williams, Lychnis, and many others will make plants strong enough to endure the winter and will generally flower next year.

POTTED PLANTS.—Those set about the grounds must not suffer for want of water. Loosen the surface of the soil in the pots and keep out weeds.

ROSES are apt to be infested by insects. Use the syringe freely, with soap suds or tobacco water. Make layers. Keep the new growth of climbers properly trained up.

SEEDS.—The finest flowers should be marked and seed collected from them as soon as ripe. Some seed vessels, such as Pansy and Phlox, scatter their seed when they burst. All such are to gathered before fully ripe, and put under a sieve to dry.

September

The borders should be bright with the gorgeous colors of the Autumn blooming flowers. These have not the tender beauty and delicate fragrance of our Spring favorites, but they come with a richness of bloom that accords with the season of ripeness and maturity. New grounds may now be laid out and prepared for Fall planting. Draining can be done and walks laid out at this season.

BULBS.—Set Hyancinths, Tulips and other spring-bloomers the last of this month or early in next. A sandy soil well enriched is best for them.

BEDDING PLANTS.—Such Fuchsias, Lantanas, Geraniums etc. as it is desired to preserve should be taken up and potted before cool nights check them.

CUTTINGS.—Provide a stock of Verbenas, Petunias, and all such things, before the plants have lost their vigor. They may be struck in pots or in a sandy border if covered with a frame and partly shaded.

GRAVEL WALKS.—These are still liable to the intrusion of weeds, and need to be raked and rolled.

LAWNS.—Sprinkle seed on bare places. Eradicate all large weeds and mow occasionally.

WEEDS.—There must be no abatement of vigilance with these until the frost stops their growth.

October

As Winter approaches, the flowering shrubs and plants in bloom become reduced in variety, so that in October dahlias, gladioluses, and chrysanthemums occupy nearly the entire field of hardy plants; yet, with proper care and taste in selecting varieties, removing all decaying leaves and other unsightly objects, and arranging for effect, these may be made quite efficient in gratifying the love of the beautiful. Attending to these, cleaning up flower borders, sowing and transplanting perennials, potting bedded plants, setting bulbs, saving seeds of late bloomers, protecting or removing tender varieties to flower pits, green-house, cellar, or window, planting shrubs, trenching and seeding, or turfing lawn, and transplanting ornamental trees, constitute the main labors of October.

BEDDING PLANTS.—Petunias, geraniums, etc., usually get so overgrown and misshapen during the Summer that they are seldom worth taking up in the Fall. It is much more satisfactory to start new plants. If this has not already been done, cuttings should be made at once.

HEDGES.—The lower shoots of dediduous hedges may now be shortened and the whole put into shape.

LAWNS.—New ones may be made. Grade, trench, or subsoil, and manure the plot. Sow clean seed early and roll and repeat the rolling before cold weather. Blue grass makes a lasting, uniform sod.

PERENNIALS.—Take up, divide, and reset Dicentra, Poeonies, Phloxes, Clematis, Hollyhocks, etc.

November

There is still work here, but it consists in clearing up and in preparation for next season. Any changes in the plan of the grounds or laying out of new improvements can be done at this season.

BULBS.—The earlier in the month these are planted the better start they will get before frost. If there are any tender bulbs yet in the ground, take up and store in a cool, dry place.

CLIMBERS.—The tender ones, like Wistaria, will need to be laid down in northern localities, and protected by a covering of earth.

EDGINGS.—Cut and trim neatly all the grass margins bordering the paths and drives, before freezing weather, and protect places where careless drivers are likely to encroach, by driving down stakes.

EVERGREENS show to the best advantage at this season of the year, after the leaves of the deciduous trees have fallen. A diversity of form and variety in shades of green, are pleasing, and can be obtained with care exercised in the selection of the plants, their location, grouping, etc., and pruning.

HEDGES.—Those of deciduous shrubs may be set now in well prepared soil. A hedge of dwarf pears planted two feet apart makes an appropriate division between a fruit and other garden, and is fruitful as well as ornamental. Clip like other hedges.

LAWNS.—Sow seed upon thin spots. Do not mow too late, else there will not be enough grass to protect the roots.

LEAVES.—As a matter of neatness it is necessary to gather these from the paths, and it is well to collect from the road-sides and elsewhere all that are at hand. They make the best protection for tender plants.

PERENNIAL WEEDS, like dock, plantain, etc., should be removed from the lawn when the ground is soft from the autumn rains. A long chisel with a handle is handy in removing their roots from the soil.

ROSES.—The tender sorts can be set in a cool pit or be heeled in and their tops covered with sandy soil or with coal ashes. Lay down the climbers and pillar roses, and cover lightly with earth.

TENDER PLANTS.—The time for taking up these depends upon the locality. If any are still out, they must be cared for. When such plants are placed in a pit or cellar they should be shut up only when necessary to protect them.

WINTER PROTECTION.—A few evergreen boughs, sufficient to break the winds, and afford shade, are found to answer the purpose of protection, avoiding the danger of smothering the plants which often resulted from the old way of covering with a thick layer of straw, closely packed about them.

December

BULBS.—It is not too late to plant now in many places, where the ground is open, but it must be done soon. Give the beds a covering of straw.

CLEAR UP, and make all as tidy as possible. The garden need not present a forbidding appearance in winter.

EVERGREENS.—The lawn on which evergreens are plentifully interspersed, and tastefully located and trained, presents a specticle that, in Winter especially, is beautiful indeed, and highly in contrast with the naked, skeleton-like appearance of other trees. The evergreens will need a little care to remove excessive burthens of snow from their branches immediately after hard storms.

LAWN.—It is not too late to give a light dressing of fine manure and ashes, leached or unleached, if needed. Rolling is also practicable and beneficial in many cases.

PROTECTION.—Give the tender roses and deciduous shrubs proper protection. The former may be laid down and covered with sods, and the latter tied up with a covering of straw. Tender evergreens must not have the straw tied too closely around them, as they are often smothered in this way. The best method is to drive stakes around them in a slanting direction, like an inverted cone, and then cover with straw, or evergreen boughs.

SHRUBS, especially evergreens that are not entirely hardy, are best protected by fastening some cedar boughs around them, or in their tops. This is the safest treatment of young evergreens, even of hardy sorts, until they become established.

SNOW should not be allowed to remain in the tops of evergreens or dense shrubs until it becomes compact and icy.

TRELLISES which are movable, should be taken down and stored under cover, those which are permanent should have a good coat of paint as a preservative.

WALKS are best made by excavating a concave bed about eight to twelve inches deep, with a ditch for draining in the center. Fill the ditch with rough stones, and also the bed to within about three inches of the surface. Then fill up with gravel and sand, and roll thoroughly. Thus made a walk will stay made.

WALL-CLIMBERS.—Protection to tender varieties may be given by making a light wooden frame to set against the wall over them, covering the frame with old carpets, or other material. Of course such vines as may be taken down and laid on the ground can be protected then with less trouble and expense.

*Other books in Donald Berg's HOMESTEAD HINTS series,
from Ten Speed Press:*

HOMESTEAD HINTS
*Find out how to cut, split, stack and measure firewood;
how to take stains out of clothing; how to build the best
bird houses and scarecrows; how to keep flowers fresh;
how to predict rain; how to plant trees; how to care for
furniture and much, much more in this compendium of
great old-time advice. "A wonderful array of old-time hints
that are still practical." — Family Handyman Magazine.
6"x9", 128 pages, $6.95, paper. ISBN 0—89815-181-3*

HOW TO BUILD IN THE COUNTRY
*The "tricks of the trade" that created last century's
picture-perfect homes can help you plan, design, build,
landscape and furnish your dream home. Use this book as
your guide to building a new home, restoring an old one or
just adding some old-time charm to any house or landscape. "Delightful...as applicable today as it was a hundred
years ago." — Country Living Magazine.
6"x9", 128 pages, $6.95, paper. ISBN 0-89815-182-1*

THE KITCHEN GARDENERS' GUIDE
Grow, harvest and enjoy a bountiful home garden with the help of dependable techniques from the days when a kitchen garden was an indispensable part of every home. "Nuggets of wisdom gleaned from 19th Century farm journals and other classic sources make this book a gem for the home gardener...an attractive and valuable missive for beginning and experienced gardeners." — Southwest Book Review.
6"x9", 160 pages, $7.95, softcover. ISBN 0-89815-201-1

You'll find these HOMESTEAD HINTS books in your library or bookstore or you can order directly from Ten Speed Press. Please include $1.00 additional for each book's shipping & handling.

TEN SPEED PRESS P.O. Box 7123, Berkeley, CA 94707

INDEX

Don Berg is an architect who's edited twelve books on yesterday's homes and gardens. He lives in Rockville Centre, New York with his wife, Christine, sons, Christopher and Teddy, and daughter, Bethany. He collected the material for this book while attempting to avoid yard work.